NEW DIRECTIONS FOR HIGHER EDUCATION

Martin Kramer, *University of California, Berkeley*
EDITOR-IN-CHIEF

Financial Planning Under Economic Uncertainty

Richard E. Anderson
Washington University

Joel W. Meyerson
Coopers & Lybrand

EDITORS

A PUBLICATION OF THE NATIONAL CENTER
FOR POSTSECONDARY GOVERNANCE AND FINANCE

Number 69, Spring 1990

JOSSEY-BASS INC., PUBLISHERS
San Francisco • Oxford

A PUBLICATION OF THE NATIONAL CENTER

FOR POSTSECONDARY GOVERNANCE AND FINANCE

Financial Planning Under Economic Uncertainty.
Richard E. Anderson, Joel W. Meyerson (eds.).
New Directions for Higher Education, no. 69.
Volume XVIII, number 1.

NEW DIRECTIONS FOR HIGHER EDUCATION
Martin Kramer, Editor-in-Chief

NEW DIRECTIONS FOR HIGHER EDUCATION is part of The Jossey-Bass
Higher Education Series and is published quarterly by Jossey-Bass
Inc., Publishers (publication number USPS 990-880). Second-class
postage paid at San Francisco, California, and at additional mailing
offices. Postmaster: Send address changes to Jossey-Bass Inc.,
Publishers, 350 Sansome Street, San Francisco, California 94104.

EDITORIAL CORRESPONDENCE should be sent to the Editor-in-Chief,
Martin Kramer, 2807 Shasta Road, Berkeley, California 94708.

Library of Congress Catalog Card Number LC 85-644752

International Standard Serial Number ISSN 0271-0560

International Standard Book Number ISBN 1-55542-826-6

Photograph and random dot by Richard Blair/Color & Light.

Manufactured in the United States of America. Printed on acid-free paper.

CONTENTS

Editors' Notes

As this volume goes to press, the U.S. economy is entering the eighth year of continuous economic expansion, apparently ignoring the supposedly immutable business cycle. Moreover, the current annual growth rate of about 2.5 percent is neither disappointingly low nor so great that it is inflationary and unsustainable. The stock and bond markets, while jittery, have recovered from the 1987 crash. The level of unemployment is at an acceptable 5.2 percent. And, the legendary Phillips curve notwithstanding, inflation seems to be in check. Furthermore, the U.S. economy is still the largest in the world by a wide margin, and our gross national product per capita is greater than that of any other country.

In spite of the abundance of current good financial news, many economists are deeply concerned about some major economic imbalances in this country and their potential effect on future prosperity. Are these discordant notes simply those of an out-of-tune instrument in an otherwise harmonious orchestra or are they a prelude to a dirge of economic catastrophe? The views of the authors in this volume are that the U.S. economy does not face an immediate economic crisis but that the concerns raised here must be taken seriously. If they are not addressed, the long-term consequences can be very dire; higher education, along with all other sectors of the economy, will face an environment that is considerably more demanding financially. In addition, our nation's financial prospects are regularly re-evaluated by the international financial markets. The discipline that these markets will impose will not necessarily be to our liking nor will it come in a predictable and orderly fashion.

Dalton and Greiner point out in Chapter Four that the federal budget is still out of control and that corrective actions that supposedly did take place were more apparent than real. Moreover, even the apparent progress has stalled. Federal debt continues to mushroom. Measured as a percent of gross national product (GNP), federal liabilities rose 62 percent during the 1980s—and this statistic does not include the considerably faster rise in off-budget borrowing. Nor was the federal government alone in this increasing dependence on debt. By the same measurement of debt divided by GNP, corporate liabilities climbed 28 percent and consumer borrowing increased 26 percent. In addition to deficit spending and the accumulating debt, the United States is importing considerably more goods than it is exporting. This trade deficit has declined from the 1986 peak (-3.4 percent of GNP), but improvement stalled in 1989 and the 1989 level (about -2.5 percent of GNP) was higher, by almost a third, than any year between 1946 and 1984.

Unfortunately, the funds made available by deficit spending, increased debt, and the trade deficit were not directed into investments in plant and equipment or into the public infrastructure. Business fixed investment (again measured as a percent of GNP) has fallen 30 percent since the 1970s. The decline in investment in the public infrastructure has been considerably more dramatic. We have used this additional cash to support a level of consumption that has grown out of line with increases in national productivity. This "over-consumption" will be brought down—but not without public and private sacrifice. And, as noted, the discipline will probably be imposed on us by the international financial markets. The necessary restraint will directly affect families, governments, and, of course, college and universities.

In Chapter One, Anderson and Massy argue that the combination of economic imbalances and possible policy miscalculations can lead to a serious multiyear recession, double-digit inflation, or both simultaneously—that is, stagflation. In the long run (five to fifteen years), they see inflation as the greater threat. While the economic consequences of rapidly rising prices are certainly debilitating, inflation brings certain advantages—not the least of which is the transfer of wealth from creditors to debtors. Such a transfer may have a seductive appeal because the United States is the world's largest net debtor. The problems that result from a serious recession, on the other hand, are considerably more palpable with fewer side benefits.

In Chapter Two, Murray observes that, in considering potential economic disturbances, planners tend to ignore the extremes because the likelihood of extreme inflation or depression is too remote psychologically. Statistically, however, the chances of severe economic perturbations are considerably higher than most of us assume. There is ample evidence for the occurrence of extreme economic conditions in our own history as well as in the histories of other nations. Nordhaus (Chapter Three) reinforces Murray's contention, citing several examples in corporate and international finance.

The primary purpose of this volume is not to simply raise the alarm of potential economic problems but to prepare higher education administrators and policymakers to anticipate and deal with these potential dislocations. In Chapter Three, Nordhaus offers a specific methodology of risk analysis. He suggests that institutional officials create a model of institutional revenues and expenditures, relating these flows to broad economic forces. The model user can then test their campus model against historical and projected economic disturbances. (As further reinforcement of the general tendency to deny risk described by Murray, Nordhaus observes that economists consistently project less volatility than history has delivered.) Using the historical data, Nordhaus estimates that large private research universities may experience "painful" shocks (that is, unexpected declines in revenues or increases in expenditures) about once every five years and that small private liberal arts colleges may feel such shocks approximately once every ten years. Although Nordhaus does not develop specific models for public institutions, his approach can be adapted readily. Estimates of exposure to economic shock in the public sector will vary by state and institutional type, but public universities may be even more vulnerable because these institutions are heavily dependent on one source of revenue and often, for structural and political reasons, have inadequate controls on expenditures. In Chapter Six, Gold points out how tightly linked state support of public institutions is to the state economy. And, of course, state and regional economies are more volatile than the national economy.

Gold, in fact, argues that state budgets can be particularly hard hit by a recession. He notes that state reserves are precariously low and that federal support of state and local programs has been scaled back considerably. Although federal support for higher education is generally not channeled through state and local governments, higher education will be competing in the state capitols more vigorously with other programs for which the loss of federal support has been devastating. He further observes that there is very little likelihood that this federal aid will be restored in the foreseeable future.

Other contributors echo this warning. Anderson and Massy (Chapter One) specifically caution institutions from relying too heavily on federal funding. In general, the authors suggest more attention to financial planning and the further development of institutional financial flexibility. They do not, however, advise college leaders to abandon long-term investment and debt strategies. This is not, in the authors' view, a time to stock canned goods in the basement, but more hard-nosed financial planning is clearly necessary.

In Chapter Five, Gurwitz explains some important changes that are occurring in the world financial markets. He suggests that many colleges and universities, because they have financial characteristics similar to financial intermediaries without all the constraints, can profit from these developments. He further observes that institutions of higher education should consider certain new "hedging" techniques. These methods are somewhat akin to increasing the deductible on an insurance policy. In effect, the institution achieves more cost-effective protection by using self-insurance against minor market fluctuations.

Dalton and Greiner (Chapter Four) offer a brief historical tour of the financial markets that further reinforces the theme of instability. But, again, there is advantage to be seized by educational institutions. These authors describe an investment strategy, strategic asset allocation (SAA), which has the potential to improve endowment returns and reduce risks. The strategy seems unlikely to improve performance if widely adopted. But, according to evidence offered by the authors, this is not the case. In spite of the successful implementation of SAA at a number of financial houses, it has not appreciably altered the overall investment strategies of balanced portfolios. There remains, in effect, a window of opportunity to improve endowment performance in the potentially unsettled markets of the 1990s.

Gold (Chapter Six) explains that there are opportunities for higher education because states look to their colleges and universities to assist in the tasks of economic development. Gold, however, warns that the evidence of success is rather slim. And, as Anderson and Massy point out in Chapter One, the real contributions of colleges and universities are felt in the long term, while too many politicians cannot look beyond the electoral cycle. This suggests a dilemma for our institutions of higher education, particularly those in the public sector. Leaders in higher education must balance their desire to be responsive to public demands and institutional needs for short-term revenues with the reality of what colleges and universities can deliver in the short term.

In the final chapter, Woolsey explains the special strains that affect policy development at the federal level and the limited attention higher education receives. It is important for leaders in higher education to understand these obstacles as they look to Washington for assistance or (at the least) policy neutrality.

The primary message of this volume is that our economy has been considerably more volatile historically than indicated in the forecasts of professional economists or in the planning assumptions of policymakers. Moreover, while the 1980s were a prosperous decade, major economic imbalances have been created in the federal budget, in international trade, and in debt levels in all sectors of the economy. Higher education leaders must be prepared to deal with potential corrective actions. These oscillations may be mild and benign, or they may be harsh and painful. Actions taken today can be critical in protecting colleges and universities should those swings be severe.

Richard E. Anderson
Joel W. Meyerson
Editors

Richard E. Anderson is a co-director of the Forum for College Financing. He is also vice-chancellor for finance and administration at Washington University, St. Louis.

Joel W. Meyerson is a co-director of the Forum for College Financing. He is also a partner and the director of Coopers & Lybrand's higher education practice.

College and university administrators should prepare for a decade or more of limited resources and a potentially convulsive economy.

The Economic Outlook and What It Means for Colleges and Universities

Richard E. Anderson, William F. Massy

While it is generally acknowledged that colleges and universities have a significant impact on the national economy (Bowen, 1977), the causal forces between higher education and the economy flow in two directions. Not only does higher education affect economic prosperity and the entire macroeconomic environment, but that environment has a direct impact on the operation of our institutions of higher learning. Moreover, the linkages are considerably tighter in the latter direction. Inflation, for example, can cause immediate disruptions on campus, while the effects from the development of a new technology or from the revision of educational standards may not be discernible for years. These macroeconomic linkages also cross national boundaries because the U.S. economy is inextricably tied to the world economy. Events in the global economy can have significant effects on our nation and on our colleges and universities.

The current macroeconomic environment is dominated by major imbalances both in national productivity and consumption and in savings and investment. Friedman (1988) offers an excellent account of how these imbalances occurred. Bergsten (1988) provides a comprehensive international perspective, and Litan, Lawrence, and Schultze (1988) consider the implications for these imbalances on American living standards. Much of the data for this chapter are derived from these sources.

Specifically, in the 1980s, the United States saved little and consumed far more than was justified by national productivity. To pay for this

NEW DIRECTIONS FOR HIGHER EDUCATION, no. 69, Spring 1990 © Jossey-Bass Inc., Publishers difference, we borrowed hundreds of billions of dollars from foreign investors. In a few short years, the United States changed from being the world's largest creditor to being the world's largest debtor. But the world money markets generally, and our foreign creditors specifically, will not finance American extravagance indefinitely. The acknowledged economic wisdom is that the international financial markets accepted the constraints of election-year politics. Beginning in the 1990s, our creditors will probably be considerably more demanding, expecting us to demonstrate that we can right our economic imbalances. Regardless of the short-term market pressures, the United States eventually must decrease consumption and increase savings. The most obvious example of these imbalances is the federal budget deficit. The structural deficit stands at a bit under $150 billion dollars, or three percent of the gross national product (GNP). (The structural deficit is the difference between federal income and expenditures that would exist if the economy were at full employment. It serves as a measure of the inappropriate imbalance between income and expenditures, with the recognition that deficit spending will often be used as a policy tool to stimulate the economy during periods of economic weakness.) This federal deficit consumes national savings and, because we must attract foreign capital to finance it, pushes interest rates higher.

The tolerance of our foreign creditors does not spring from charitable motives. Because of the composition and magnitude of international trade, the prosperity of all nations is increasingly interdependent. How effectively these imbalances are corrected is important to all our trading partners. It is in this international context that macroeconomic policies are made. Whatever choices are ultimately selected will have tremendous impact on American higher education.

The purpose of this chapter is to sketch some plausible scenarios, identify their probable consequences for colleges and universities, and suggest what we should be doing to protect ourselves. Other chapters in this volume consider specific topics. It is natural for individuals to assume that the current environment will last well into the foreseeable future. However, as Nordhaus argues in Chapter Three, individuals tend to systematically underestimate risk. In Chapter Two, Murray considers some of the economic extremes that can occur and suggests implications for colleges and universities. Nordhaus reviews a model he has constructed that allows institutions to assess their vulnerability to changes in the macroeconomic environment. In Chapter Five, Gurwitz explains how higher education financial managers can adapt financial hedging techniques used by financial intermediaries. In Chapter Four, Dalton and Greiner share their concern about economic imbalances expressed in this chapter, although they differ from us in their conclusion about the prospects for a sustained inflationary period. Dalton and Greiner suggest an approach to investing endowment assets that should produce above-average returns during a volatile economic period. In Chapter Six, Gold reviews the state public policy environment. Woolsey reviews the significant limitations on federal policymakers and the relatively limited attention higher education receives.

The Most Likely Scenario

The single best guess about the economic outlook is for generally favorable conditions with moderate growth and inflation—in other words, a continuation of the stable expansion trajectory we have enjoyed since 1982. The Stanford inflation forecast for the next several years is in the 4-4.5 percent range, and the consensus of most economists is for growth of about 2.5 percent. (This consensus existed when this chapter was written but there are acknowledged perils. By the time the volume is published or as the reader reviews the material, a new consensus may have developed or we may even be in the middle of a recession or inflation.) Real interest rates will probably remain around 4 percent, with the dollar and unemployment rate fairly stable.

Sustaining this growth will not be an easy task and will involve real sacrifice. To simultaneously maintain economic growth and satisfy our foreign creditors, the U.S. economy must shift from one based on domestic consumption and government spending to one based on exports. In turn, such a transformation requires several simultaneous policy successes. Business investment must grow to continue the manufacturing expansion that has already begun. To increase business investment, the federal budget deficit must be cut to avoid "soaking up" savings. Any significant reduction in the federal deficit will require a combination of spending cuts and tax increases. At the same time, the dollar must remain weak unless our export products become intrinsically more attractive to foreign purchasers. (Some assert that the dollar must decline an additional 20 to 25 percent against the yen to eliminate the trade imbalances.) The sum of these changes—less federal spending, more taxes, more business investment, a weak dollar, more exports, and fewer and more expensive imports will, by force of arithmetic, reduce the amount of GNP that is devoted to current consumption. Bergsten (1988) estimates that, even if we avoid a recession, growth in domestic consumption must be held to 1-1.5 percent per year—this compares with a growth of almost 5 percent per year in domestic demand since 1983.

The political and economic obstacles to achieving these goals are considered in the Alternatives Scenarios section of this chapter. However, the successful implementation of these policies has direct implication for our colleges and universities. Both the flagging living standards and the need for our economy to grow out of our debt will put tremendous pressure on policymakers to increase productivity and reduce public expenditures.

Effects on Higher Education. The quest for productivity improvement will help colleges and universities by increasing the demand for research and development and for education of the labor force, especially in scientific and technical areas. Support for student aid will also continue, but the policy rationale will probably shift. Although student financial aid has traditionally been supported on the grounds of both equalizing opportunity and bringing the poor into the productive economy, the projected slow growth in living standards may noticeably shift the policy balance toward the pragmatic and economic role. Middle-income families are likely to become increasingly discontented with slower growth in disposable income. Their support for subsidies for the poor may wane unless these monies can be shown to have benefits that will "trickle up." We may, as a consequence, face a growing federal interest in measuring student progress and degree achievement. Furthermore, as state budgets become squeezed, all public expenditures will be reviewed with growing rigor and we should certainly expect state interest in accountability to accelerate.

In spite of the positive role that higher education can play in improving national productivity, the urgency of the deficit reduction will limit funding for new federal programs and make it difficult even to sustain current ones. Our problem is that the contribution of higher education is only seen in the long-term view and the politician's view is relatively short term. With a government that seems quite willing to mortgage its future on a massive scale to sustain current consumption, our concerns about the long-run health of the academic enterprise will be very difficult to sell. Effective public relations must be a major component of our efforts to sustain the financial health of colleges and universities. To complicate the problem further, while we feel so vulnerable, we look so rich (see Kennedy, 1988).

The most immediate dangers for higher education stem from the urgent need to end the era of massive budget deficits and the effect of past deficits on our standard of living. The deficit pressures will directly conflict with George Bush's stated goal to be the "education president." For example, a delegation of presidents and chancellors from the American Association of Universities (AAU) met with President-elect Bush on December 5, 1988, and reported that he "reemphasized his oft-stated commitment to education, while asking for understanding of the budget restrictions he faces. The president-elect also emphasized a need to look more to the private sector for R&D support. He said that stronger initiatives are needed in this area, but implied that no changes would be made in the tax code."

Another concern for private institutions is the prospect of greater resistance to tuition increases from those who perceive themselves to be worse off because of lower real wages, higher taxes, or loss of federal student assistance. Pressure on prices will not be limited to instruction. The overhead rates of research universities are already under siege from federal agencies and principal investigators (Massy, 1990). This will get worse as research funding tightens. State budgets will also be affected by efforts to reduce expenditures at the federal level, and this will limit funding possibilities for many public institutions, although the impact will be mitigated by the size and diversity of the individual state environments.

Perhaps the greatest danger comes from efforts to "enhance" tax revenues without raising the general tax rates. Congress has already been working on stricter definitions of unrelated business income, and further restrictions could limit the revenue-generation capacity of both public and private institutions. Private institutions are probably more vulnerable to tax-enhancement efforts because of their greater dependence on charitable contributions and their political independence. The deductibility of gifts was curtailed by the Tax Reform Act of 1986, and the possibilities for additional curtailment abound. The same is true for tax-exempt bonds issued by private institutions—the $150 million cap may be lowered. Even more ominously, the Tax Reform Act of 1986 termed the bonds issued by private colleges and universities "private activity" bonds. At that time, however, these institutions were spared from inclusion in the state uniform volume cap—an omission that is too easily undone. If private college bonds were included in the state volume cap, access to the tax-exempt bond market would be almost eliminated for most private colleges and universities. But the most frightening prospect of all is the Treasury Department's proposal to place a 5 percent excise tax on the investment return of private college and university endowments. This would cost dearly and make it all but impossible for these institutions to sustain current programs and provide the capital needed for such established federal priorities as improved science facilities. It would also tip the precarious competitive balance between private and public institutions in favor of the public institutions.

Alternative Scenarios

The scenario of continued growth conceals formidable policy tensions and some significant dangers for colleges and universities. The policy problems are both economic and political, and they must be resolved both within our shores and abroad. A major economic challenge will be to raise our lagging productivity growth. Productivity in the United States and related trends compose an enormously complex subject. Conclusions are affected by what is measured, the start and end points, and the corrections applied to the data. The United States is still the largest and most productive country in the world. A major factor for our recently "lagging" productivity growth is that other countries are catching up. In a world made considerably smaller by major improvements in communications and transportation, this equalization was inevitable. Still, our low rate of investment has surely contributed to the decline. In addition, the recently reported improvements in productivity may also be situational—caused by the rapid decline in the dollar, which boosted exports and manufacturing and agricultural outputs. Productivity in finance, insurance, and other services (with the probable inclusion of education), however, declined between 1981 and 1986 (*Economic Report of the President,* 1988).

Many economists believe that we will need to increase GNP growth to 3.5 percent if we are going to "grow our way out of the deficit." But this increase will be hard to achieve given that the economy is now near capacity and that business investment during the 1980s was low by both international and historical standards. (From 1982 onward, business investment averaged only a little over 2 percent of national income and in no year achieved our historical average of 3 percent. The figures for Japan and most European countries are considerably higher.) Furthermore, to maintain growth at even the 2.5 percent level for the intermediate future, we must avoid a recession. But policymakers will fight future contractions with one hand, perhaps both hands, tied behind their backs. The typical tools for fighting a business slowdown are monetary and fiscal. In the threat of a recession, the classic response by the Federal Reserve Board is to increase the money supply and reduce interest rates. This stimulates consumer demand and business expansion. However, a major reason that interest rates are high now is that we must attract sufficient capital to fund our deficit. The second policy is fiscal—deficit spending by the federal government. Again, our profligacy has boxed us into an uncomfortable, if not untenable, corner. Prospective increases in the deficit to stimulate the economy can shake investor confidence, exacerbating any downturn.

The political obstacles are no less formidable than the economic ones. To restore confidence in the dollar and rebuild our economic strength, we must reduce both the budget and trade deficits. The former requires higher taxation and lower government spending, and the latter means that more of the goods we produce must be shipped abroad. Reduced domestic consumption is not the type of news that politicians like to bring back to the voters.

As if these difficulties were not enough, we cannot raise exports and reduce consumption without the cooperation of our major trading partners. In particular, Germany and Japan (major exporters) must realign their economies for further domestic consumption. If this policy coordination is not achieved, there may be a glut of goods on the world market, creating an international recession.

The scenario of sustained expansion may be most likely, but it is nonetheless highly tenuous. As explained above, the fiscal and monetary tools cannot solve all policy problems at the same time. Furthermore, the hoped-for transition to a structurally balanced budget requires complex policy adjustments that can be error prone. The Federal Reserve Board must anticipate the tightening of fiscal policy by just the right lead time and exact amount, and financial markets must see the easing of monetary policy in the right light (and have confidence that the deficit actually will be reduced). Failure anywhere in the chain can trigger recession, inflation, or both.

Recession. Some potential causes of recession are listed in Exhibit 1. What follows a recession depends on factors like the speed of propagation of the downturn, associated defaults or bankruptcies, the efficacy of the policy responses, and the policies of our trading partners. Under one scenario, propagation is so fast that prices fall precipitously for commodities and assets like stocks and real estate before there can be any policy intervention. Interest rates plummet, but since nominal rates cannot drop below zero, real rates become very high relative to the falling price level. (This is the "liquidity trap" described by Keynes [Dimand,

Exhibit 1. Recession Scenarios

Recession can be triggered by any of the following:

1. The Business Cycle. The expansion is six years old, and the economy is at capacity; faster expansion requires higher interest rates to constrain investment demand, leading to a classic downturn.

2. Budget Balancing. In an effort to restore market confidence, the federal government takes serious steps to reduce the federal budget deficit, but these measures are too severe and a recession follows.

3. Protectionism. Reducing the federal deficit and trade deficit simultaneously requires that our trading partners export less and import more. For a variety of reasons particular to their own political environments, they may not make this change. If trade barriers grow and world trade slows, a worldwide recession can follow.

4. Flight from the Dollar. Foreign creditors lose confidence that the United States will get its economic house in order and withdraw from the U.S. debt markets. The Federal Reserve Board raises interest rates to protect the dollar (a diving dollar only exacerbates the situation), causing consumption and business investments to fall.

5. Defaults. There are at least three groups of potential debt problems: thrift institutions, corporations newly capitalized with "junk bonds," and "lesser developed countries" (LDCs). If defaults by any one of these sets of debtors get out of control, the loss of wealth and financial confidence can undermine the financial markets, reducing investment and consumer confidence, and (as a consequence) aggregate demand.

1988] to explain the causes of depression.) The loss of wealth plus high real interest rates chokes off demand, causing more failures and bankruptcies, and bankruptcies become more likely because of high corporate debt levels. Unemployment soars, and we have a truly deep recession. Furthermore, the effects are probably transmitted abroad due to the tight coupling of international trade and the financial markets.

The policy response to this situation is, of course, to provide large amounts of liquidity and stimulate aggregate demand by raising government spending and reducing taxes—a response that will not be long in coming. We certainly know too much to repeat the errors of 1929-1933, when the deepening recession triggered efforts to balance the federal budget and increase interest rates. (Dimand [1988] provides a fascinating account of how classical economic theory and the conventional wisdom of the day drove policy precisely in the wrong direction.) Problems of international cooperation can hinder these policy interventions, but there is little doubt that the worst consequences will be mitigated and that a repeat of the Great Depression will be avoided even in this "catastrophic case."

Inflation. The more likely result of a policy response to a threatened economic downturn is that the Federal Reserve Board will act at the first sign of trouble, thus preventing a severe downward spiral. This is what happened in the days following October 19, 1987. The biggest danger in that response is overshooting the mark, thus triggering a round of inflation some months later. Widespread defaults, bank failures, bankruptcies, and high unemployment are simply not tolerable in economic or political terms. The Federal Reserve Board then has little choice but to run the risk of erring on the side of easy money. Any loss of confidence on the part of foreign lenders would drive the dollar sharply downward because increasing interest rates would not be an option. In the longer run, we would have to rely on the lower dollar to aid our trade balance and permit the sale of U.S. assets at bargain prices. But the weak dollar may not bring much relief if other countries erect trade barriers to protect their own industries.

The causes of inflation summarized in Exhibit 2 are certainly not unlikely. Few people want inflation. However, in assessing its likelihood, we must remember that inflation has advantages (despite the fact that any move in an inflationary direction will surely produce a swift negative reaction in the financial markets). Consider these points: (1) Inflation transfers real wealth from lenders to borrowers—and the United States has become the largest net borrower in the world. (2) Inflation moves people up in the tax brackets to the extent that brackets are not completely indexed. (3) Inflation generates "capital gains" and increases the spread between historical and replacement cost depreciation. (4) Inflation creates opportunities for reducing real wages without the trauma of low-

Exhibit 2. Inflation Scenarios

Inflation can be caused by any of the following:

1. Policy Error. The Federal Reserve Board errs on the side of liquidity and low interest rates. This may occur as part of its normal operations or, more likely, result from a too aggressive corrective reaction to a sharp downturn.

2. Flight from the Dollar. Foreign investors withdraw from the U.S. debt market, driving the dollar down in spite of attempted policy interventions. The higher import prices trigger a round of inflation.

3. Commodity Price Shock. External events cause the price of an important commodity to rise precipitously, setting off a series of price increases. Disruption in oil production caused by the OPEC cartel or perhaps a Middle Eastern conflict is the most obvious candidate.

4. Political Relief from Debt and Budget Problems. Politicians, responding to a public chafing under heavy debt and related tax burdens, ineluctably accede to inflationary policies.

ering nominal wages. All four points have been recognized by economists, going at least as far back as Keynes (see Dimand, 1988).

If We Fall, Which Way? The United States faces enormous challenges: flagging productivity growth, a seemingly intractable federal budget deficit, stagnant domestic investment, an apparent addiction to foreign debt with its service requirements, and an unfavorable trade balance. Politicians and policymakers must answer to a restive electorate, but past excesses have given foreign creditors a good deal of control over our destiny. The economic policy problems facing the United States have been described as an extraordinarily dangerous "tightwire act." The slightest overcorrection in one direction or the other could bring disaster. In response to a downturn, will we act too late with too little and bring about a severe recession? Or will the policy hand be too heavy and unleash inflationary forces?

Sadly, the tightwire metaphor is too comforting because it implies that the fall will be in either one direction or the other. We may be visited by recession and inflation simultaneously, and college and university financial managers should be on guard against various combinations of recession and inflation. However, our best guess is that inflation represents the greater long-run threat. Recession is certainly possible at any time. Indeed, it may be more likely than inflation in the short run. But recessionary threats are often dealt with swiftly, quite possibly at the risk of triggering inflation. When all is said and done, inflation's causes are more popular with more people than is the preventive medicine, however unpleasant the prospective discipline of the financial markets may be.

Our policymakers will try sincerely to avoid inflation, but if it comes to a choice between inflation and recession, inflation will win. We do not believe that the strong anti-inflation policies of the Volker years are likely to be repeated under today's conditions. That medicine is too dangerous because of the size of our foreign debt and, more important, the perils posed by our excessively leveraged corporations, the struggling lesser-developed countries, and the fragility of many thrift institutions. In all probability, we will experience a period of renewed inflation—perhaps even double-digit inflation and some of the debt relief that it will bring—before we will accept recession in return for price stability.

Implications for Colleges and Universities

These economic winds will be felt throughout our institutions of higher education. They will affect curriculum, personnel, and enrollment policies, as well as financial management. This discussion and the following chapters, however, will focus primarily on financial matters (see *Capital Ideas*, 1988, for a brief review of curriculum and policy issues.)

What can college and university financial officers do to blunt the negative effects of deficit reduction and the prospect that we will experience inflation, recession, or both? There are strategies that can make a difference. Indeed, strategic thinking has never been more important than at present, and all institutions are vulnerable. Public institutions, with heavy dependence on state spending, must be prepared to live with the vicissitudes of that support. Recent reports suggest that the squeeze on state budgets has already begun ("As 1989 Legislatures Convene . . . ," 1989). Although private college support will be more stable, it will not be any more abundant. Incomes may not keep pace with college costs, and the downward spiral in savings rates will erode family financial reserves. Equally important, labor force participation by women has risen dramatically in the last few decades (*Economic Report of the President*, 1988, pp. 289–290). In the coming years, fewer families will have a reserve worker waiting to enter the labor market to help support the family during the years of higher college-tuition payments. The private research university, which has always seemed unshakable, may be particularly vulnerable with its heavy dependence on federal research support, tuition, and investment income.

The strategies considered in this chapter fall into four broad categories: current operations, capital for facilities and equipment, investments, and public image. The model constructed by Nordhaus in Chapter Three shows that the greatest effects of economic events on private research universities are in program support and investment return. The effects of price changes on operating costs tend to be balanced by corresponding changes in operating revenues (other things being equal). The following strategies are consistent with that view.

Strategies Related to Current Operations

1. Avoid optimistic income forecasts, particularly income to be derived from the federal government (such as indirect cost recovery), invest-

ment earnings, and gifts. Be alert to the possibility of increased price resistance from tuition payers and the federal research sponsors.

2. Avoid heavy forward commitments, especially those that depend on anticipated income growth. Be prepared to retrench quickly if income growth turns down or the actual level of income declines.

3. Establish cost-containment programs to reduce the need for future tuition and overhead rate increases. These should include processes for enhancing productivity in both academic and administrative areas and harvesting the results as cost savings (that is, as opposed to quality improvements).

4. Maintain or create budget flexibility to respond to initiatives that a sluggish economy will force on higher education. Funds may be needed to build more elaborate cooperative ventures with industry, specifically to assist in the transfer of technology to the manufacturing sector. Improving elementary and secondary education is also likely to become a higher priority issue. Public institutions may, of course, go to their legislatures and request extra funds, and private institutions may ignore these demands/opportunities altogether. But there will be strategic advantages to institutions in either sector that have the flexibility to respond swiftly to emerging societal needs.

Strategies Related to Capital for Facilities and Equipment

5. Develop detailed plans for sources and uses of capital, and stick to them. The need for expenditures on facilities and equipment is great, but sources of capital cannot be taken for granted because of the pressures on state budgets, increasing competition for philanthropy, and the high cost of debt. While long-term debt is advantageous during a period of sustained inflation, debt service can be difficult in an environment characterized by income instability. Moreover, current high real interest rates presumably fully discount prospective inflation.

6. Minimize institutionwide capital costs and, for public institutions, the state's overall cost of capital. Avoid using cash for a capital project that qualifies for tax-exempt financing while using taxable debt for another project.

7. Fully integrate capital budgeting with financial forecasting of operations. Make appropriate provision for the transfer of unrestricted funds as needed by the capital budget. Also, include projected debt service and operations, maintenance, and utilities for new buildings in the operating forecasts. Similarly, projected growth in research volume and related revenue, as well as expenditures associated with the new facilities, must be fully integrated into future plans. Failure to forecast these costs and revenues accurately is serious anytime but especially so in times of financial stringency. The integration of operating and capital budgets can result in decisions to defer building projects that might be affordable solely on the basis of capital considerations.

8. Use hedging techniques, as appropriate, to minimize risks. See Chapter Five by Gurwitz.

Strategies Related to Investments

9. Minimize long-term fixed-income investments. Maintain a sufficient position in high-quality long bonds to put a floor under endowment yield during a sharp recession. However, the potential for transferring wealth from lenders to borrowers during a period of unexpected and sustained inflation makes this a dangerous time for bondholders. The issue is whether current high real interest rates fully reflect inflationary risks. Modeling of the Stanford endowment and budget suggests that a 15 percent allocation to long bonds provides the desired minimum "yield insurance." Stanford has structured a "ladder discipline" wherein fifteen-year Treasury bonds are held for five-year periods on a staggered basis.

10. Sufficient working capital in "money market" funds is desirable for several reasons. It provides "yield insurance" as discussed above and raises current return (compared with many equity assets). It also protects against the downside risks of both inflation and recession while providing a source of funds to take advantage of special investment opportunities created by volatile markets.

11. Continue to invest in equities and real estate to obtain a solid return coupled with inflation protection. In spite of the current investment risks, the endowment must be managed with a long-term perspective. For example, shopping centers with percentage rents and office buildings with inflation-protected leases are particularly attractive. The latter also can be a useful hedge against recession, provided the leases are long and with low-leveraged blue-chip clients.

12. Avoid highly leveraged investments such as certain real estate deals and leveraged buy outs. These will be particularly vulnerable during a recession and must be avoided.

13. Diversify internationally to hedge uncertainty with respect to the dollar and the domestic economy. Such diversification will be particularly important if the United States fails to deal adequately with the deficit.

Strategies Related to Public Image

As mentioned earlier, colleges and universities are extremely vulnerable to adverse policy decisions at the federal or state level. We expect fair treatment, or even special consideration, because we are engaged in "public service." However, too frequently higher education is perceived to be just another self-interest group. All our policies, including financial ones, can have adverse consequences in this unstable financial environment. We must be extremely cautious, in efforts to strengthen the financial bases of our institutions, not to offend public and legislative sensibilities.

Because of this political vulnerability, we offer the following additional recommendations:

14. Use caution in generating unrelated business income. The small-business community has become increasingly concerned about unfair competition from nonprofit organizations and specifically from colleges and universities. Even paying associated taxes will not quell the criticism if we take unfair advantage of our captive markets or fail to show appropriate sensitivity to small businesses that rely on our students and staff as customers.

15. Do not abuse tax-exempt status. Dimensions of this issue range from relations with local governments to the sale of tax advantages. Our increasing relations with the corporate world will undoubtedly open up new possibilities for gain that may be offensive, even though they are completely legal.

16. Use tax-exempt debt prudently. Most of the obvious abuses have been shut off by the Tax Reform Act of 1986. However, no legislation is 100 percent effective, and we are probably more vulnerable to perceived abuse here than anywhere else. The institutional volume cap may be extended to public institutions, or private institutions may be included under the state uniform volume caps.

17. Avoid overly aggressive investment policies. The current criticism of university endowment participation in leveraged buy outs can increase. Even heavy overseas investments may be attacked as un-American.

None of these strategies call for budget reductions, but rather they are aimed at the more effective management of program growth, the diversification of investments, and the avoidance of highly optimistic or leveraged positions in either area. Also, they take into account a political environment that is likely to be dominated by economic issues—one in which politicians will need little excuse to decrease expenditures or to increase short-term public revenues.

The adoption of these strategies will not guarantee that institutions will emerge unscathed from whatever may happen in the larger economy. But they should help.

Summary

The macroeconomic environment will probably be extremely volatile in the 1990s. This is an important time for colleges and universities to conserve capital for use on facilities and equipment and to provide investment return for future operating subsidies. It is certainly no time for policies that dissipate significant amounts of capital through current operating deficits, however strong the immediate program claims. Nor is it a time for investments that fail to consider the possibility of either a sharp recession or, particularly, a sustained inflation. This is a watershed time when the future of many institutions can be profoundly affected by current financial policy decisions.

Correcting the economic imbalances of the past eight years will dominate public decisions well into the 1990s. America's colleges and universities will be called on to assist in raising U.S. productivity and to tighten our belts and use resources as prudently as possible. But prudence is likely to be defined differently by college administrators, by public officials, and by families. We must be alert to these discrepancies and make our case for continued public and private support as forcefully and as clearly as we can.

References

"As 1989 Legislatures Convene, Public Colleges in Many States Face Tough Battles for Funds." *Chronicle of Higher Education,* January 4, 1989.

Bergsten, C. F. *America in the World Economy: A Strategy for the 1990s.* Washington, D.C.: Institute for International Economics, 1988.

Bowen, H. R. *Investment in Learning.* San Francisco: Jossey-Bass, 1977.

Dimand, R. W. *The Origins of the Keynesian Revolution.* Stanford, Calif.: Stanford University Press, 1988.

Economic Report of the President. Washington, D.C.: U.S. Government Printing Office, 1988.

Forum for College Financing. *Capital Ideas.* New York: Teachers College, Columbia University, 1988.

Friedman, B. M. *Day of Reckoning.* New York: Random House, 1988.

Kennedy, D. "How Can We Look So Rich, Yet Feel So Poor?" Paper presented at the Los Angeles Alumni Conference, Stanford University, Stanford, Calif., March 1988.

Litan, R. E., Lawrence, R. Z., and Schultze, C. L. (eds.). *American Living Standards.* Washington, D.C.: The Brookings Institution, 1988.

Massy, W. F. "Funding Research." In R. E. Anderson and J. W. Meyerson (eds.), *Financing Higher Education in a Global Economy.* New York: Macmillan, 1990.

Richard E. Anderson is a co-director of the Forum for College Financing and vice-chancellor for finance and administration at Washington University, St. Louis.

William F. Massy is vice-president for business and finance at Stanford University and a professor in Stanford's graduate schools of business and education.

*The range of risks facing colleges and universities extends well
beyond a modest inflationary period or a short recession.*

Considering the Extremes

Troy Y. Murray

If planning is the assessment of the future consequences of present decisions, it must include an understanding of potentially extreme changes
in the operating environment. Of particular interest to financial managers is evaluating the economic contexts of their decisions and the possible
effects of major economic dislocations. Although extreme dislocations
are not likely, they must be considered as possibilities.

The cornerstone of implementation of a long-term asset-allocation
plan for colleges and universities is a hedge against economic disaster.
There are two extreme cases that should be considered: hyperinflation at
one extreme and a 1930s-style collapse at the other.

Although hedging against economic disaster may be more common-
place in long-term investment planning, college and university financial
offices should recognize that the effects of economic catastrophe will not
be limited to the endowment fund but will extend to most aspects of
institutional life.

From mid-1929 through mid-1932, when prices declined a cumulative 20 percent, the real (inflation-adjusted) return on stocks was –76
percent and dividends declined by 70 percent. Bonds, however, increased
43 percent and, if of high quality, continued to provide a stream of
income to their holders. Bonds are the only asset class that protects the
capital value and the stream of income of financial assets in that kind of
catastrophe. Even today, the strongest argument in favor of always holding some bonds in one's portfolio is as "insurance" against deflation.
What percentage to hold will depend on how much "insurance" a Board
of Trustees thinks it needs.

At the other extreme is unanticipated, rapidly accelerating hyperinflation. The worst cases of this—the sort experienced in recent years in Mexico and South America—have not been experienced in this country in this century. On several occasions, during and after World War I, following World War II, and for sixteen years from 1966 through 1981, however, we have experienced rates of inflation well above the historic mean. Some insurance against this lesser form of catastrophe is needed.

From 1978 through 1981, for example, prices increased a cumulative 51.5 percent. In that same period, stocks showed a real return of 4.6 percent, while bonds experienced negative real returns of -24.2 percent. High quality, income-producing real estate, by contrast, returned a real annual rate of 27.6 percent. As prices increased, owners were able to raise rents.

Thus, while the argument for real estate as the optimal inflation hedge may not be as clear as the case for bonds as a deflation hedge, some "insurance" against this extreme should also be part of every institution's portfolio, whether that insurance be real estate, asset-rich common stocks, or precious metals.

As we consider this kind of hedging in the context of investment planning, should we also be thinking in similar terms for our institutions' operational plans? It is unlikely that there are comparable "insurance" policies available to protect institutional operations and finances against either of these catastrophes. Instead, the best hedge may be to consider both these extremes regularly in an institution's plans. By assessing at both staff and trustee levels the institution's risk (measured in terms of the likely effects of economic disaster), the college or university can identify the possible responses to disaster as well as the probability of the occurrence of any particular disaster.

To take one case, because the experience of the 1970s and early 1980s is indelibly etched in institutions' memories, colleges and universities are perhaps better equipped to think about hyperinflation. Consideration of this extreme case now, in advance of its occurring, may help to avoid some of the mistakes made in the 1970s, including the following:

• Widespread reluctance for several years to raise tuition and fees commensurate with increases in the Consumer Price Index
• The false sense of security engendered by high yields on stocks and bonds, while asset purchasing power was being steadily eroded
• With the rest of society, consuming and borrowing instead of saving and investing.

As the recent Coopers & Lybrand report on deferred maintenance suggests (Rush and Johnson, 1988), colleges and universities will still be paying the price in the 1990s for the inflation of the 1970s and their response to it.

We do not have the same vivid memory of the Great Depression that our parents and our grandparents do. Unable to draw on the wisdom gained through experience, colleges and universities may be incapable of estimating the likely effects of another significant depression, because they are not able to profit from the mistakes made the last time around. A limited review of colleges and universities suggests that the campuses were relatively insulated from the devastating effects of the Great Depression (see Kelly, 1974; Miller, 1966; Cary, 1962; Stadtman, 1970). Indeed, Derek Bok (1988) recently remarked that Harvard did just fine through the 1930s.

This seeming indifference may be due in part to the nature of the catastrophe: Although inflation is an embezzler, deflation is more of a mugger. Although colleges and universities will pay for a long time for the mistakes made in periods of extreme inflation, the effects of deflation and the responses to it are more immediate and direct.

In another significant depression, enrollment is likely to fall (at least at private institutions), gifts and appropriations are likely to decline, and the cost of certain goods and services is likely to decrease. For some items, such as room and board, colleges and universities may be forced to reduce prices. Some have suggested that the Great Depression has been replaced by a series of rolling, regional deflations that have successively struck the Midwest, the Mountain states, and Texas in the 1980s. The higher education analogy may be the successive "enrollment depressions" that are striking those institutions that have been unprepared for the ever worsening demographic trends.

The degree of risk in deflation is tied to the fixed nature of the liabilities of a college or university. In the 1930s, institutions often reduced wages and salaries for clerical and operations personnel while holding faculty salaries constant. With today's more highly organized work force, this same flexible response may not be possible.

Instead, a deflation in the 1990s may threaten financial aid and the need-blind admissions policies. Another fixed obligation, and a liability that did not exist or was not as prominent in the 1930s, is the long-term debt of a college or university. If the economy collapses and a university is unable to refinance its debt at lower interest rates, the fixed nature of this liability could have a severe effect on its overall financial condition. Recognizing this exposure, some institutions are hedging themselves by increasing their use of variable-rate debt.

In summary, the experience of investment planning demonstrates the value of protecting the endowment fund against the risks of economic catastrophe. If disaster strikes, however, its effects will not be confined to the endowment but will be felt throughout the college or university. Although there may be "insurance policies" available to hedge the institution's investments against these extremes, contingency planning may be the best protection available for the rest of the assets.

References

Bok, D. Paper presented at the symposium "Higher Education in a Changing Economy," Boston, October 5, 1988.

Cary, H. W. *The University of Massachusetts: A History of One Hundred Years.* Amherst: University of Massachusetts, 1962.

Kelly, B. M. *Yale, A History.* New Haven, Conn.: Yale University Press, 1974.

Miller, R. E. *Light on the Hill: A History of Tufts College 1852–1952.* Boston: Beacon Press, 1966.

Rush, S. C., and Johnson, S. L. *The Decaying American Campus: A Ticking Time Bomb.* A joint report of the Association of Physical Plant Administrators of Universities and Colleges and the National Association of College and University Business Officers. Boston: Coopers & Lybrand, 1988.

Stadtman, V. A. *The University of California 1868–1968.* New York: McGraw-Hill, 1970.

Troy Y. Murray is a managing director at Cambridge Associates. His background is in financial planning and management control.

*Administrators can and should evaluate the specific exposure
of their institutions to economic risks.*

Evaluating the Risks
for Specific Institutions

William Nordhaus

No one who has studied the finances of the academy doubts that there is
an academic business cycle not dissimilar to the conventional business
cycle. But is it possible to estimate the magnitude and sources of the risks
faced by colleges and universities? Anderson and Massy (Chapter One)
reviewed the threats to the economy and the implications for college and
university financial management. In Chapter Two, Murray urged administrators to protect themselves from the risks of extreme economic dislocations. This chapter offers a method of risk analysis by which colleges
and universities can evaluate their vulnerability to a number of financial
and economic factors, including the inflation rate, wage levels, stock
prices, long-term interest rates, government spending, and national
productivity.

Before I launch into the discussion, I will explain why a risk analysis
is useful. Those who study human behavior have found that, with striking regularity, people underestimate the degree of uncertainty that they
face. For example, when people are asked to give both their opinion and
their subjective degree of uncertainty about "encyclopedia questions"
(questions to which the answers are known), people tend to underestimate their ignorance. The counterpart of this in business is the tendency
to ignore unpleasant but unlikely outcomes. For example, those who lent
almost a trillion dollars to developing countries seemed to ignore the

This chapter is a nontechnical summary of a longer background paper that
explains the sources and methods used for the results presented here (Nordhaus,
1988). A copy of the longer paper is available on request from the author.

likelihood of a massive default—even though defaults had occurred during the 1930s and would be predictable in a tight-money recession. Risk analysis could have shown the possibility of a severe downturn in oil and real estate and might have led bankers to be more prudent in the early 1980s.

In practice, careful risk analysis is rarely performed. Businesses routinely forecast the "most likely" outcome for sales, costs, profits, and so forth. Examinations of the upside and downside risks in a systematic fashion are almost never done. The purposes of this chapter are to suggest a methodology for performing systematic risk analysis, to apply this methodology to higher education, and to assess both qualitatively and quantitatively the macroeconomic risks of colleges and universities.

The actual mechanics of the risk analysis models are omitted in this nontechnical explanation. Two models are developed: one for a selective private university (with a medical school) and one for a selective private liberal arts college. A general description of these models is presented in the text, followed by a discussion of the financial flows of colleges and universities, the variance of those flows, and the financial risks colleges face from external economic events.

Approach to Risk Analysis

Risk analysis begins with the selection of the "endogenous" and "exogenous" variables. Endogenous variables are affected by the model, while exogenous variables are outside the model. The components of college and university income and expenditures are the endogenous variables. Measures of the larger economic environment are the exogenous variables. The purpose of the exercise here is to determine the potential effects of variations in the economic environment on net institutional income.

Constructing the Model. The first step is selecting the variables. A list of the basic endogenous and exogenous variables used in this analysis is given in Table 1. (A more complete set of variables with definitions is provided in Nordhaus, 1988.) After the variables are selected, the relationship between the endogenous and exogenous variables is estimated. For example, the university model is built on the assumptions that the bulk of grant and contract income (80 percent) is determined by the general level of federal spending and part of this income (20 percent) is determined by general economic activity. Student-aid expenditures are estimated to be a direct function of enrollment and tuition. Although the full list of variables (and the model) could certainly be expanded, they serve to illustrate the method.

Separate estimating equations for income and expenditures were established for both the college and the university models. The two income and expenditure equations were then combined by dividing total

Table 1. A Short List of Variables

Endogenous Variables	Exogenous Variables
Income	Federal spending
Endowment and gifts	Gross national product
Grants and contracts	Inflation
Medical services[a]	Interest rates
Tuition	Stock prices
Expenditures	Tuition level
Faculty salaries	Wage rates
Material and supplies	
Staff compensation	
Student aid	

[a] Only applies to university models.
Source: Nordhaus, 1988.

income by total expenditures. For mathematical convenience, these equations are put in logarithmic form. Both models assumed fixed enrollments. For most institutions, enrollments are subject to fluctuation (that is, they would be exogenous variables). In those cases, the model would need to be considerably different from the ones constructed here. Moreover, public institutions are primarily dependent on state spending and, consequently, on the health of the state economy; models of publicly supported institutions must reflect this dependence.

Most modeling efforts attempt to forecast the expected value of the endogenous variables—in this case, the expected ratio of institutional income to expenditures. Risk analysis, in contrast, is concerned not only with the expected value or "most likely" outcome, but also with some measure of the risk or dispersion of the variables of interest. There are several ways to consider this dispersion, including a full graphic presentation of the range of outcomes. In this review, however, only the mean and the standard deviation of the variables are estimated.

If the probability distributions for the economic variables and the relationships between those measures and institutional income and expenditures were well established, it would be straightforward to generate the probability distributions. In most cases, those relationships are not well established, and the future values of the economic variables are unknown.

The problem has been simplified here in two ways. First, the structure of the estimating equations are represented by greatly simplified financial models of a university and a small college. Although these stylized models do not exactly represent the finances of any particular institution and both are models of private institutions, they are sufficiently simple that they can easily be modified to fit the finances of most public or private institutions. Second, the probability distribution of the economic variables is determined from historical data. Variables such as growth of gross national product (GNP) or interest rates appear to have sufficiently stable behavior over time, and their future uncertainty can be reasonably estimated by looking at their historical behavior.

To summarize the methodology, simple models of the finances of a private university and a private college were created with economic data taken to be exogenous. The distribution of these economic variables (for example, inflation and wage levels) is estimated from historical data to obtain an estimate for the expected value of the endogenous variables (for example, tuition income and endowment income). The penultimate endogenous variable is the ratio of institutional income to expenditures. But, as this analysis is also interested in change in the institutional variables, the mathematical "derivative" of this equation yields the final form. With the full set of assumptions and mathematical manipulations (available in Nordhaus, 1988), the university model is reduced to the following form (brackets indicate rates of change):

1. $$[x] = 0.1[m] + 0.13[q] + 0.4[b] + 0.06[r] + 0.21[g] - 0.55[w] - 0.25[f] - 0.16[p]$$

where

$[x]$ = change in the ratio of income to expenditures
$[m]$ = rate of change in stock prices
$[q]$ = rate of change of inflation-adjusted GNP
$[b]$ = rate of change in inflation-adjusted tuition charges
$[r]$ = change in interest rates
$[g]$ = rate of change in discretionary government spending
$[w]$ = rate of change in wages
$[f]$ = rate of change in faculty salaries
$[p]$ = rate of inflation.

Equation 1 helps to show the vulnerability of colleges and universities to different forces. Five forces work in a favorable direction:

- The stock market through its impact on the value of endowment
- The economy through its impact on giving and contracts
- The escalation of tuition and other fees above the rate of inflation
- Higher real returns on the fixed-income portfolio
- Higher discretionary government spending.

The following three forces are the identified negative forces:

- Increases in wages over the general price level
- Escalation in faculty salaries
- Higher inflation.

The coefficients of the university equation give a rough idea of how variation in different forces affect the finances of higher education. They indicate, not surprisingly, that private universities are quantitatively most sensitive to changes in tuition level, along with movements in real wages and faculty salaries. In addition, the government budget plays a significant role, as do financial returns and inflation.

Using an identical approach but different proportions of income sources and expenditures, we can configure the reduced form of the model for a private liberal arts college as shown in equation 2. (The definitions are the same as listed for the university model of equation 1.)

2. $$[x] = 0.1[m] + 0.05[q] + 0.45[b] + 0.06[r] + 0.14[g]$$
$$- 0.60[w] - 0.35[f] - 0.16[p]$$

A comparison of equations 1 and 2 shows the difference between the areas of vulnerability of a research university and those of a private liberal arts college. The university is affected somewhat more by shocks to the overall economy and to government spending. The college is more heavily influenced by variables that are idiosyncratic to higher education, such as the escalation factors in faculty salaries and tuition charges. But the major influences are surprisingly similar for both types of institutions.

However, the risk of the different forces cannot be judged without an estimate of the variability of each variable. The quantitative risk is the product of the "vulnerability coefficients" in the equations times the respective risks (potential fluctuations) of the individual variables. The next section estimates the risk associated with each variable.

Riskiness of Each Factor. Analyzing the riskiness of each factor in both equations requires an examination of the medium run exposure. The period used in this analysis is three years. I first will discuss briefly how the variability of each factor can be estimated.

Two sorts of data are examined to calculate risk: First, forecasts of Data Resources, Inc. (DRI) for the economy are reviewed. (DRI was chosen because it is the most systematic of published forecasters in presenting its results and in considering alternative scenarios.) Examining the variability of the different variables across different DRI scenarios provides an estimate of the relative volatility of those variables included in the DRI model. Second, we examine the relative volatility of the different variables over the postwar period. Here, we simply look at the movement of the relevant variable and evaluate how much it has moved in recent years. The data are shown in Table 2.

Discussion of Uncertainties. Two major conclusions follow from the analysis of variability. First, the historical data show significant change in the underlying volatility of the data over time (see Nordhaus, 1988).

Table 2. Risks in Different External Factors[a]

Factor	Factor Risk[b]		
	DRI[c]	Historical	Assumed
Stock market prices	—	21.1	21.1
Interest rate	9.40	18.9	18.9
Government	0.67	16.3	16.3
Real GNP	1.40	4.3	4.3
Real wages	0.69	2.1	2.1
Price level	0.39	7.0	7.0

[a] Percent forecast error or uncertainty, three-year horizon.
[b] The factor risks represent the volatility of the underlying factor, measured as the uncertainty of the factor over a three-year period. For example, a forecast of the stock market is assumed to have an uncertainty of 21 percent over a forecast horizon of three years. A more complete discussion is contained in Nordhaus, 1988.
[c] DRI = Data Resources, Inc.

For example, interest rates appear to be around twice as variable in the 1970–1987 period as they were between 1954 and 1969. This finding conforms to changes in the conduct of monetary policy, which became much more active and willing to induce major changes in interest rates, particularly during the 1979–1982 period. In addition, inflation and price level became more unstable in the 1970s and 1980s, which was the period of the oil shocks and major changes in the dollar-exchange rate. Government spending on goods and services became less volatile from 1970 to 1987. The variability of other variables appears to have changed relatively little. Stock prices were marginally more volatile—largely because of 1987. Output and real wages showed no major change in volatility over the period.

Comparison of the DRI forecast risks with the historical variability shows that the risks estimated by using DRI data have no systematic connection to the historical volatility. Every variable displayed has lower risk than would be justified on historical grounds. The differences are modest in the cases of interest rates and real GNP—where the understatement is one-half to one-third. But the differences are enormous for price level and government spending, where the variabilities are understated by a factor of 20.

Given the difference between the DRI forecast risks and the historical data, it seems useful to interpret the DRI risks as "scenarios," that is, as plausible paths that might be followed under conditions of tight money or fiscal compromise. However, it seems unlikely that these scenarios can be usefully employed to describe the full set of risks faced in the macroeconomy.

Because of the likelihood that the DRI estimates of risk are not based on historical risk data, the following analysis will, therefore, rely instead on the risk estimates from the historical data. But the failure of the DRI risks to approximate historical risks underscores the contention at the beginning of this chapter that economic agents (even highly sophisticated and successful forecasters like DRI) not only underestimate the degree of uncertainty but also do not appear to pay systematic attention to the historically proved risks inherent in their business.

Estimates of Risks for Higher Education

The estimates of risk can now be used to evaluate the impact of different external economic events on higher education. The basic technique is the following: The weights of the most important factors affecting the finances of higher education are analyzed. Then, the inherent risk attached to each factor is estimated. Finally, the weights of the factors with the risks of each factor are mathematically combined to obtain the "impact of economic uncertainties" on higher education.

Overall Risks. Table 3 shows the estimates of the weight or importance of the different factors. ("Weights" are derived numbers. When the mathematics are complete, the weight of each factor is simply the coefficient of that term in the final equation.) Column 2 shows the weights for our model research university derived from equation 1, while column 3 shows the weight for our model small college derived from equation 2.

Table 3. Weights and Total Impact of Different Risk Factors

1	2	3	4	5
	Weight of Factors[a]		Total Impact[b]	
Factor	University	College	University	College
Stock market prices	10	10	2.1	2.1
Interest rates	6	6	1.1	1.1
Government	21	14	3.4	2.3
Real GNP	13	5	0.6	0.2
Real wages	−55	−60	1.2	1.3
Price level	−16	−16	1.1	1.1
Total			4.1	2.7

[a] Percent of total income or expenses. The weights in columns 2 and 3 are the share of the factor in income or expense, in percent, as shown in equation 1 in the text for small universities or equation 2 in the text for small colleges.
[b] The total impact in columns 4 and 5 is the product of the weight of the factor and the volatility of the factor (the latter is shown in the last column of Table 2). (The product is divided by 100 to be expressed as a percent.) The units of the impact are in standard deviations of the logarithm of the income-expense ratio. Therefore, the standard deviation of the income-expense ratio for universities over a three-year horizon is 4.1 percent.

The last two columns in Table 3 show the calculated impact of risk for both universities and colleges. The last row in Table 3 shows the total risk.

To compute the "impact" for each factor and for the total, multiply the intrinsic volatility or risk of each variable (shown in the last column of Table 2) by the weight shown in Table 3, and then divide the result by 100 to express it as a percent. The product of volatility and risk is the total impact. For example, the stock market is estimated to have an inherent volatility of 21.1 percent per three-year period; the stock market is found to have a weight of 10 percent in the budgets of our model institutions; therefore, the overall impact of the stock market is $(21.1 \times 10) \div 100$, or 2.1.

To explore the interpretation further, look at Figure 1, which shows the movement over time in the income-expense ratio for both colleges and universities (using a logarithmic scale, which is useful because the slope is always the rate of growth of the series in question). Examine the estimated curve for research universities, shown as the solid line in Figure 1. During the period from 1954 to the mid-1960s, the external factors were extremely favorable, as is shown by the rapid growth of the income-expenses ratio. From the mid-1960s to the early 1980s, the trend was basically neutral, with sharp drops in the late 1960s, the early 1970s, and the early 1980s. In the last three years examined, 1985–1987, the external factors were relatively unfavorable because of trends in government spending and a decline in stock prices.

The long-term trend for colleges is less favorable over the period, although the short-term trends look quite similar to those for universities. The major difference between small colleges and research universities lies in the contribution of government, particularly support for the life sciences, which has contributed significantly to the financial growth of research universities through rapid growth of support for biomedical research.

Figure 1. Trend in the Total Potential Impact of Financial Factors Affecting Colleges and Universities

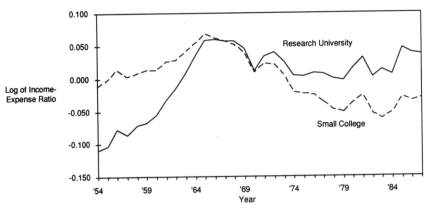

Figure 2 shows the forecast errors (historical risks) faced by these two types of institutions. This graph indicates the annual rate of growth of the income-expense ratio. When the rate of growth is positive, a favorable shock has occurred to the income-expense ratio. A negative number, representing a negative rate of growth, is an unfavorable development for colleges and universities. In regard to the units used, a value of 0.050 in Figure 2 signifies a 5 percent favorable shock to the income-expense ratio—that is, the budget has a 5 percent surplus over what a straight extrapolation would provide. A value of -0.025 implies a 2.5 percent unfavorable shock (a budget deficit of about 2 percent of income or expenses relative to trend. Figure 2 shows the same trends as Figure 1 does, namely that events were generally favorable from the mid-1950s to the late 1960s and generally unfavorable from the late 1960s to the mid-1980s.

Another way of examining the risk is to look at the distribution of forecast errors of the change in the ratio of income to expenditures. In other words, how often will a university face major positive or negative shocks? (The estimate of that frequency is based, of course, on historical data.) Table 4 shows the frequency of shocks of different sizes for the historical period 1954–1987 for both research universities and small colleges. Table 4 shows that research universities experienced unfavorable (negative) shocks of more than 5 percent of the budget in 2 of 34 years, and unfavorable shocks of between 3 and 5 percent of the budget in 4 of 34 years. Small colleges were less severely hit, experiencing unfavorable shocks of more than 3 percent in only 2 of 34 years.

How "large" are the shocks that are analyzed here? A rough guess is that a shock to the income-expense budget of 3 percent or more will be quite painful. For example, in a college or university with a budget of $100 million, this shock would require income increases or budget cuts

Figure 2. Volatility of Economic Factors Affecting Colleges and Universities

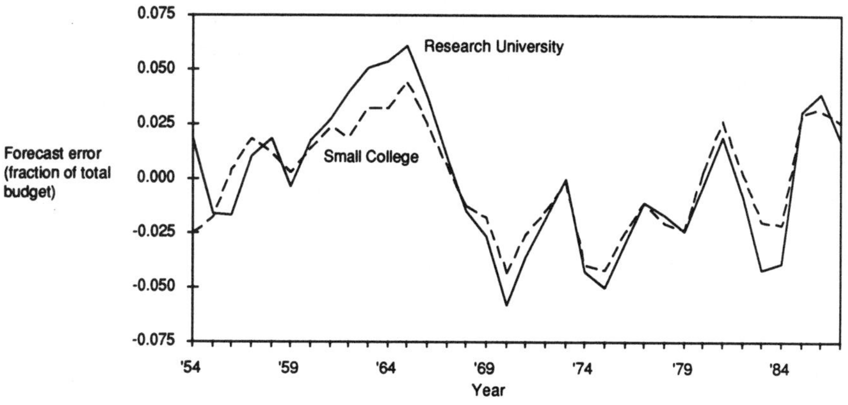

Table 4. Frequency of External Shocks to Colleges and Universities[a]

Size of Shock	Research University	Small College
More than 5%	3 years	0 years
3% to 5%	2	5
1% to 3%	9	8
-1% to 1%	5	7
-3% to -1%	9	12
-5% to -3%	4	2
Less than -5%[b]	2	0
Total	34 years	34 years

[a] Historical frequency (in number of years) from 1954 through 1987.
[b] "Less than -5%" means an *unfavorable* shock of more than 5%.

Source: From calculations of the forecast errors of the logarithm of the income-expense ratio.

of around $3 million in order to balance the budget. So, for a small college, a shock of 3 percent would require raising tuition levels about 4 percent more than trend or would require a cut in staffing of approximately 6 percent. On the basis of experience at Yale and similar institutions, staffing cuts of 5 to 10 percent are extremely painful for the institution, while increases in the tuition rates of 3 to 5 percent above trend raise a loud howl from alumni, students, and their families.

How often will such large shocks occur due to external events? The historical data suggest that unfavorable shocks of 3 percent or more will occur in approximately one of every five years for large research universities and in one of every ten years for small colleges. The painful reactions discussed in the previous paragraph will then be required unless provision has been made for the inherent risks.

Risks from Different Sources. This analysis is designed to estimate not only the inherent financial risks to higher education, but also to examine the risk that comes from individual factors.

Table 3 shows risks associated with different factors in columns 4 and 5 and in the first six rows. In addition, these results are shown graphically in Figure 3 (for our model research university) and in Figure 4 (for our model small college). Each figure shows three bars for each factor and for the total. Starting from the left, the bars in the chart for each factor represent:

- The "weight" of each factor = the relative importance in the budget
- The "volatility" of each factor = the extent to which a particular factor is unpredictable
- The overall "impact" of the volatility of each factor on college and university budgets.

A number of results stand out from the figures and tables:

Figure 3. Weight, Volatility, and Impact of the Economic Factors Affecting Private Universities

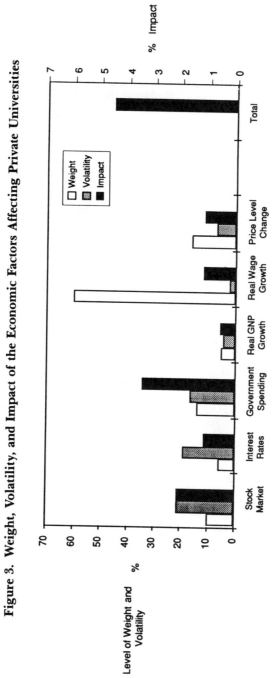

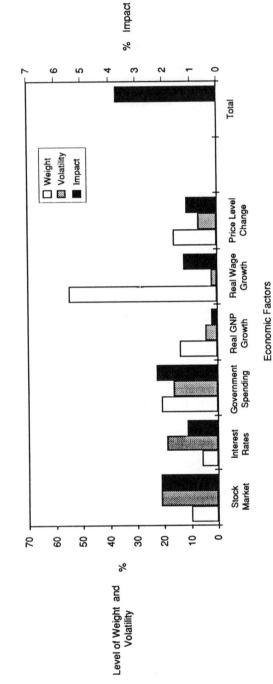

Figure 4. Weight, Volatility, and Impact of the Economic Factors Affecting Private Colleges

• Table 3 shows the great volatility that comes from the government budget. This conclusion will not be surprising for public universities, who are used to "legislative risk," but it may come as a surprise to private universities. The reason for the great inherent risk from the federal government is not only that a large part of the budgets of higher education are derived from the federal government, but also that this has been a highly volatile spending stream. It may well be that the period ahead, as the federal government confronts its large deficit in a serious way, is a period of particular risk to higher education.

• The risk from financial markets are well known to colleges and universities. These risks come from the inherent volatility of stock and bond markets. Many universities tend to "smooth" the uncertainties by calculating the income from endowment according to a weighted average of past market values. This smoothing will make the year-to-year adjustments to financial-market volatility less painful, but they will not remove the long-run need to adjust.

• The impact of wages and the price level (or inflation) is intermediate on colleges and universities. Wages have the potential of being extremely important risks, because they constitute such a large share of expenses; fortunately, they are relatively stable and predictable and therefore pose only minor financial risk. Inflation has often been held to be the bugaboo of higher education, but its impact may have been overestimated. For the most part, both income and expenses of colleges and universities move with inflation, so there is little real impact of inflation on higher education. The major impact can be the loss of buying power if endowment income erodes in inflationary periods.

• Finally, it is surprising how little direct impact the business cycle, through real GNP growth, has on colleges and universities. On reflection, this could have been predicted for two reasons. First, GNP turns out to be relatively predictable over the medium run (even though it may have large elements of unpredictability in the short run). Second, many colleges and universities are remarkably insulated from the business cycle. Most top-rated universities are not demand-constrained; unlike automobile manufacturers or department stores, the level of "output" of colleges and universities is determined by internal, nonpecuniary considerations and is affected neither by small changes in the real incomes of households nor by the exchange rate on the dollar.

It should be recalled that the risks analyzed here pertain only to those variables that are external to higher education. The impacts of changes in the tuition charges and of the escalation of faculty salaries have been ignored. These were omitted for two reasons. First, they are at least in part under the control of higher education and therefore cannot be taken as exogenous to university decisions. That is, they are typically decision variables rather than external factors in university finances. Second, the tuition income and the escalation of faculty salaries adjust to the finances of higher education. If the finances of higher education are strained, this will tend to put upward pressure on tuition charges and tend to depress faculty salaries. So there is an element of self-adjustment in tuition and salary escalation.

Conclusion

This analysis has attempted to evaluate systematically some of the major economic risks facing institutions of higher learning. We started by constructing budgets of a stylized small college and research university, and then we analyzed major economic factors affecting those budgets. The major external factors considered were real GNP, the stock market, interest rates, federal government spending, inflation, and real wages.

Next, we looked at historical volatility (or unpredictability) associated with each major external variable, along with the compound uncertainty associated with the factors that were determined externally (exogenous factors). On the basis of historical data, it was estimated that major unfavorable shocks (greater than 3 percent of the budget) would occur one year in five for major research universities, and one year in ten for small colleges.

In the analysis of the major uncertain factors, the largest surprise was the importance of uncertainty about the federal budget to private colleges and universities. This concern is most important for research universities (particularly those with large research programs and medical schools). The overall impact of the potential volatility of government spending overshadows all other external influences. The next largest potential factor is the stock market, followed by interest rates, inflation, and wage trends. For small colleges, the uncertainty associated with government spending is also the most important single factor, although the stock market and other variables are close behind.

The analysis undertaken here has at least two important implications for the management of educational institutions. The first implication involves forecasting. Once the important risks have been identified, colleges and universities can track them carefully to get early warnings of future trouble. It is important for institutions to track federal budget trends along with other major economic variables.

The most important implication, however, is that institutions should prepare for foul economic weather. The appropriate reaction of institutions to their risks is a problem that takes us far afield from the current topic, although the type of reaction clearly is related intimately to the risks that institutions run. In one sense, the risks are analogous to the risks of bad weather in the agricultural sector. There are two kinds of response to bad harvests: anticipate them by building a grain stockpile or adjust to them afterward by cutting food consumption. Similarly, colleges and universities can anticipate future financial shocks by accumulating surpluses and retaining budgetary flexibility, or they can adjust to unfavorable shocks by having periodic financial crises and budget cuts after unfavorable shocks occur. Prudence should lead to anticipating shocks by building in flexibility or storing financial reserves much as we store grain for years of drought. In deciding on the appropriate stockpiles, however, one must carefully estimate the risks inherent in the economic environment.

Reference

Nordhaus, W. "Finanzangst: What Are the Financial Anxieties of Colleges and Universities?" Presented at the symposium of the Forum for College Financing, National Center for Postsecondary Governance and Finance, Annapolis, Md., November 3, 1988.

William Nordhaus is John Musser Professor of Economics at Yale University. From 1986 to 1988, he was provost of Yale. Nordhaus also served on President Carter's Council of Economic Advisers.

In spite of the economic uncertainties, college and universities must invest for the long term. Certain techniques can reduce the risks and increase the returns.

Investing in an Uncertain Economic Environment

Timothy Dalton, Kenneth Greiner

In a book about making difficult economic decisions, one risks overemphasizing the perils and neglecting the opportunities. To balance the picture, in this chapter we will suggest a way of thinking about the investment environment of the 1990s and an approach for investing in an unsettled financial environment. The approach, *strategic asset allocation*, is a generalized method for allocating assets in a portfolio. Although strategic asset allocation is conceptually appealing and has received a fair amount of public attention, it is still not widely practiced. Consequently, there are still opportunities to "add value" to portfolio management with the technique.

Most approaches to asset allocation are essentially extrapolations of long-term trends. In reality, however, there are substantial divergences from the historic returns of the major asset categories. And these divergences can persist for several years. Economic, financial, and valuation cycles—and the interactions with each other—play important roles in determining absolute and relative returns to the various assets. Most important, in the current environment, investors must be able to evaluate the responses by the administration, Congress, and the Federal Reserve Board to the expansive monetary and fiscal policies of the 1980s. Their decisions will have an important impact on inflation, the dollar, interest rates, real economic growth, and profits. In addition, both stocks and bonds delivered double-digit returns through most of the 1980s. Consequently, interest rates—both nominal and real—are much lower and equity valuations are much higher than just a few years ago. In this

New Directions for Higher Education, no. 69, Spring 1990 © Jossey-Bass Inc., Publishers

potentially unstable environment, college and university endowment managers must be cautious, and appropriate portfolio balance is especially
important.

The High-Cholesterol Economy

The economic imbalances discussed at the 1988 Annapolis Symposium
persist. These troubling distortions characterize a nation living beyond
its means:

- We save much less than previous generations
- We borrow more and faster than income growth would justify
- We import more than we export
- We milk the public treasury for more government-provided goods and
  services than it collects from us in taxes
- We underinvest in productive plant and equipment
- We neglect our aging public infrastructure
- We borrow huge sums abroad to finance this profligacy.

Much of this deterioration is a product of the 1980s and a corollary of
our fiscal and monetary policies of the last eight years. The major goals of
the incoming Reagan administration in 1980 were to strengthen our
nation's military capabilities, reduce the intrusions of government in our
daily lives, and significantly cut the tax rates for individuals and corporations. These were all worthy goals and were, in large part, fulfilled. Unfortunately, as with most commendable objectives, there were costs. A number
of factors—the fiscal mix of our defense buildup, tax cuts, and the rapid
growth of entitlement programs—have left the federal budget woefully
out of balance. Since 1980, the government has borrowed over $1 trillion
and its indebtedness has risen from 26 percent of gross national product
(GNP) to 42 percent, as shown in Figure 1. (Although the federal debt
was at higher levels in the early 1960s, those liabilities were a heritage
from financing World War II and the Korean War. The debt buildup we
are currently experiencing is unprecedented in peacetime.)
Living beyond one's means has not been limited to Washington, as
Figure 1 shows. Expansive fiscal and monetary policies, combined with
seemingly limitless credit, encouraged a binge of buying and borrowing
by the American consumer. Real consumer spending rose by 25 percent
from 1980 through 1987, while real incomes advanced only 20 percent.
The flip side of spending more, of course, is saving less: The personal
savings rate has fallen by 50 percent since the 1970s.
Corporations have also been piling up debt in the 1980s. Despite a
30 percent drop in net business fixed investment relative to GNP, business
indebtedness rose dramatically. Instead of investing in productive plant

**Figure 1. Debt as a Percentage of GNP:
Consumer, Government, and Corporate**

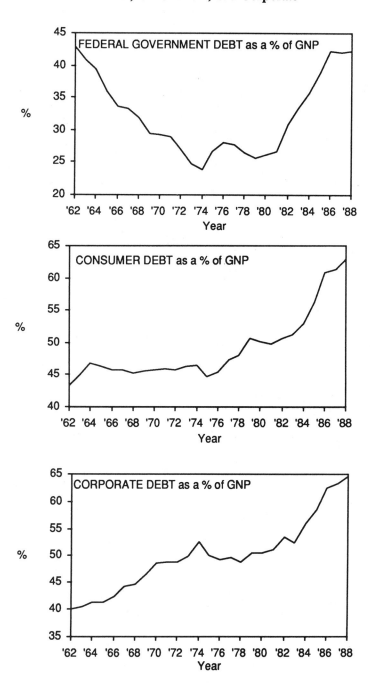

and equipment, corporations have preferred to purchase undervalued assets—either through acquisition of other companies or repurchase of their own shares. Moreover, it has been advantageous to borrow most of the purchase price rather than use one's own cash or exchange shares. Consequently, the ratio of interest expense to cash flow increased from 16 percent in 1986 to 22 percent just two years later.

There was much to cheer about our economic progress in the 1980s. Inflation and interest rates fell precipitously. Employment growth in the United States was the envy of the world, and unemployment dropped to its lowest level in fifteen years. Capacity utilization crossed 85 percent, and corporate profits and cash flow rose sharply. These accomplishments, however, were fueled largely through current consumption—both in the private and public sectors—and the bill will be paid by our children and grandchildren. We have borrowed heavily from the future to satisfy our desires today.

The Bush administration has inherited this legacy of economic instant gratification. Although it may be comforting to look back at the accomplishments of this decade, a look into the 1990s produces a prodigious list of challenges. We must take the following steps:

• Significantly reduce the federal deficit
• Increase the net private savings rate, at least to the level of the 1970s
• Eliminate the current account deficit
• Eliminate the dependence on foreign capital
• Increase the investment in plant and equipment to a share of GNP equivalent to the average of the 1970s
• Decrease the growth rate of borrowing in the United States below the growth rate of income.

In short, the United States has dramatically reduced its investment in the future. Private savings have declined from 8 percent of GNP in the 1970s to 4.5 percent in 1988. The total of federal, state, and local government deficits has climbed from 1 percent of income to 2.1 percent over the same period. Consequently, total net savings available to fund private investment declined from 7 percent of GNP in the 1970s to 2.5 percent in the 1980s. To make up for this savings shortfall, it has been necessary to attract substantial sums from abroad. Foreign capital inflows amounted to a net $140 billion in 1988, and have totaled about $500 billion since 1981. This substantial reduction in net domestic savings and the substitution of foreign capital are the major reasons that real interest rates are so high at the close of the 1980s.

Investment in productive plant and equipment has suffered as well. Even with the surge in capital spending over the past two years, business fixed investment accounted for only 2.3 percent of GNP in 1988; this was

30 percent lower than the 3.3 percent average in the 1970s. Consequently, our capital stock has fallen from 106 percent of GNP in 1982 to 91 percent in 1987. As we enter the 1990s, our capital stock is at its lowest level since World War II.

In addition, as shown in Table 1, the growth rate in the stock of public capital (what we spend on roads, bridges, dams, and so on) has fallen to less than 1 percent. In 1965, the United States devoted 4.4 percent of GNP to public investment; the amount decreased to a paltry 1.2 percent in the 1980s.

Why all the fuss? It really is quite simple—increases in private and public investment tend to increase productivity. Workers become more productive when they have better equipment. The message in Figure 2 is striking, because it tests the theory across international borders. Among the industrialized nations, Japan has invested more per worker and, predictably, has the highest growth rate in productivity. Conversely, the United States is at the bottom of the productivity ladder, and its investment per capita was the lowest over that same period.

Our productivity must improve. Over the past decade, the anemic growth in output per worker has suppressed wage growth to a rate no greater than that of inflation. As measured by real wage growth, the standard of living of the American worker has not improved for ten years.

Poor productivity growth impairs the ability of American businesses to compete internationally. The faster productivity grows, the less prices have to rise to achieve a desired level of profitability. And, obviously, the lower the price, the more competitive the product.

A substantial increase in private and public investment, relative to both GNP and the labor force, is essential to this country's long-term economic health. Failure to raise investment ensures the gradual erosion of real wages and the dollar—and our standard of living.

After the stock market crash of 1987, the clamor about the federal budget deficit reached such levels that it appeared that serious reductions might be achieved. In 1989, as the stock market climbed ever higher, the federal budget deficit often was dismissed as an insignificant problem.

Table 1. Net Business Investment and Productivity

Period	New Business Investment (% of GNP)	Growth Rate of Private Capital Stock (%)	Growth Rate of Public Capital Stock (%)	Growth Rate of Productivity (%)
1950–1980	3.3	3.8	3.5	2.0
1980–1987	2.4	2.5	0.9	1.3

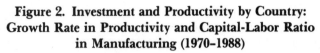

**Figure 2. Investment and Productivity by Country:
Growth Rate in Productivity and Capital-Labor Ratio
in Manufacturing (1970–1988)**

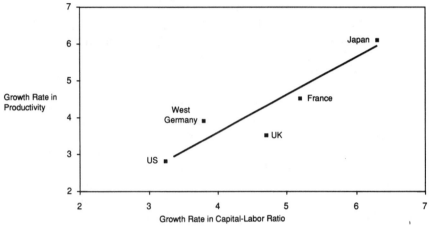

Since the budget shortfall had dropped from $220 billion (5.2 percent of GNP in fiscal 1985) to $155 billion (3.2 percent of GNP in 1988), it was clearly less of a concern. Although everyone is cheered by this trend, deficits of such magnitude are still a huge problem demanding serious attention.

There are a number of reasons that the real federal deficit may be considerably higher than the official figure. Notably, the Social Security surpluses provide about $60 billion in additional revenue that should be saved and not spent. In addition, the federal government has significantly increased guaranteed federal loans (such as Stafford loans) and the debt issued by government-sponsored enterprises (that is, the farm credit system). The total debt in these two categories rose from $425 billion in 1980 to over $1.2 trillion in 1988. The advantage of this debt to federal legislators and the administration is that technically it does not count as a federal liability. This technicality notwithstanding, not all this debt will be collectable. And a recession could raise the costs of guaranteeing these loans by tens of billions.

Two important reasons support our unrelenting concern about the federal shortfall. First, by mid-1989, the deficit had apparently stopped declining. Second, our deficit, unlike the shortfalls of some of our trading partners, is still absorbing a huge portion of private savings.

In the spring of 1989, the administration estimated that the fiscal 1989 shortfall would be $170 billion, up from $155 billion in 1988. How could this have happened if the Gramm-Rudman-Hollings legislation called for a deficit of only $136 billion? All that law requires is that the administration and the Congress agree to a projected deficit within $10 billion of the legislated target at the outset of the fiscal year. If the actual shortfall is, say, $40 billion higher than projected, the law still would not have been breached. This may be a dangerous piece of legislation because it provides the nation with a false sense of comfort and the impression of an ongoing, mandated, steady decline in the deficit. But, in fact, there are absolutely no penalties for missing the targets as long as the Congress and the administration can agree on projections that meet the law. In August 1988, for example, the Office of Management and Budget (OMB) forecast a fiscal 1989 deficit of $129 billion on the basis of a spending increase of 3 percent. As this chapter is being written, the OMB was projecting a deficit of $170 billion on the basis of an 8 percent increase in outlays.

While all the above may explain partially why progress in reducing the deficit has been stalled, these facts still do not answer the arguments of those who claim the deficit is not much of a problem. In fact, the U.S. deficit by itself does not seem so bad; its percentage of GNP is lower than that of several other industrialized nations, including Japan. But a major problem with government deficits is their absorption of savings. If the private savings rate is around 20 percent, as it is in Japan, then a deficit of 3 or 4 percent is not of much concern. However, the private savings rate in America fell from 8 percent of GNP in the 1970s to 4.5 percent in 1988. Since the deficit of all levels of government combined in the United States was 2.1 percent of GNP, then savings were equivalent to only 2.4 percent of income available to finance the much needed investment in productive plant and equipment, business inventories, and housing. This level of net savings is clearly insufficient and contrasts sharply with the 7.1 percent rate that prevailed in the 1970s in the United States. Even though the deficit may not be a problem when viewed in isolation, it is a major concern for a nation whose private savings rate has halved in ten years. To say that it does not matter is to say that high real interest rates are fine, that the nation can tolerate continued underinvestment in plant and equipment, and that heavy reliance on foreign capital is acceptable.

The sad tale in Table 2 shows deteriorating private savings, generally increasing public budget deficits, a drop in business investment, and the emergence of foreign capital inflows.

It is tempting to wring one's hands and talk about the inevitable fall of the United States into irreversible decadence. However, we have too much faith in the market mechanisms of the capitalistic system. Largely because of the pressure from market participants, policymakers will be forced, albeit begrudgingly and slowly, into adopting a fiscal and monetary mix that will reverse this spend-borrow-and-pay-later mentality. We need more savings, less consumption, and a lower deficit. These goals can only be achieved by fiscal and monetary stringency and changes in the tax code that favor savings and penalize consumption.

A modest decline in the dollar and slower growth in final demand

Table 2. Users and Providers of Capital in the United States

	Capital Users					Capital Providers		
Period	Net Business Fixed Investment (%)	Inventory (%)	Residential Invest-ment (%)	Federal, State & Local Deficit (%)		Net Private Savings (%)		Foreign Capital Inflows (%)
1970–1979	3.3	+ 0.8	+ 2.8	+ 1.0	=	8.1	+	0
1980–1987	2.4	+ 0.4	+ 2.0	+ 2.7	=	5.9	+	1.8
1988	2.3	+ 0.8	+ 2.2	+ 2.1		4.5	+	2.9

Note: Small differences in the totals of rows 1 and 2 are due to rounding errors.

would allow the reduction in the trade deficit to continue without creating severe inflationary pressures. A higher savings rate and a declining deficit would allow real interest rates to fall and also lessen our dependence on foreign capital. Meanwhile, above average growth in production and lower real interest rates would encourage much needed investment by our nation's business sector, thus paving the way for meaningful productivity growth. Deferring current gratification for the sake of a higher standard of living for one's children has been an integral American value. There is no reason to assume that sacrifice is dead forever.

Again, our optimism on this score follows from our belief that periodic beatings in the markets will push policymakers in sensible directions. Investors will not keep scooping up our newly issued debt if they feel that these imbalances are permanent features. Of course, the markets always clear, but not necessarily at the same price. The odds are quite good that investors, foreign and domestic alike, will express periodic alarm over policy intransigence and vote with their feet. Then, progress most likely will follow market panic.

As we write this chapter, we are quite concerned that the markets are particularly vulnerable to disappointment. Honeymoons are meant to elicit enthusiasm over the future. Mr. Bush's optimism and the nation's acceptance of his promises are in keeping with this tradition. However, there may be an uncomfortably large gap between rhetoric and reality. The twenty years of increasingly accommodative monetary policies have produced a secular increase in inflation, which soared to double digits, peaking in 1980. The rapid and unexpected increase in inflation created economic, financial, and personal havoc. Ultimately it was market pressures—primarily in the currency and bond markets—that forced an end to the easy money policies of the prior decades. In short, the Federal Reserve Board had no choice but to limit the growth of the money supply to avoid a run on the dollar and to keep the bond markets from collapsing. The current actions of investors, consumers, and businessmen reflect a lingering sensitivity to and fear of inflation. We believe this sensitivity will help keep inflation in check. However, it is prudent to expect periodic episodes of rising prices and to anticipate market reactions to fiscal and monetary policies.

Given the prospect for unsettled capital markets, college financial managers must be especially cautious in selecting investments. Traditional rules of thumb are likely to be poor guides to action in the 1990s and beyond.

Implications for Managing University Financial Assets

In the first chapter of this volume, Anderson and Massy assert that college financial managers must continue investing for the long term and that their investments should tilt toward equities, including stocks, real estate, and natural resources. Certainly we agree with that general assessment, but portfolio managers must select from within those investments and determine the relative tilt between equities and fixed-income securities. Moreover, if the investment time horizon is shortened a bit, it may be more appropriate to put more funds in fixed-income investments.

   Strategic Asset Allocation. One approach to portfolio management is strategic asset allocation (SAA). In using SAA, a portfolio manager reviews various asset categories against their historical performance. Then, after considering the relative valuations of those assets against both historic norms and the current economic and financial environment, the manager shifts assets within the portfolio into categories that are undervalued. This shifting may tend to be automatic and formula driven, or it may be more judgmental.

   The case for active asset allocation rests on the assumption that one can either enhance returns without creating too much volatility or reduce volatility without sacrificing too much return. We argue that there are opportunities to substantially alter the asset mix of college endowments in order to achieve either of these two objectives. Moreover, a skillful use of SAA can enhance returns and reduce variability simultaneously.

   Beyond simply improving returns to standard investments, SAA expands investment options. The spectrum of asset possibilities has exploded in the 1980s. One can choose from real estate, timberland, precious metals, U.S. small company stocks, and securitized automobile loans. And, as the global economy is shrinking, financial managers must be capable of placing investments across international borders. Those who fail to understand the revolution of cross-border and cross-instrument investing are doomed to endure inferior investment results. SAA is an important tool for expanding portfolio breadth.

   The Case for Strategic Asset Allocation. The complete investment arena is too broad and complex for discussion in this chapter. A case for active asset allocation can be made, however, by examining past returns for domestic stocks, bonds, and short-term fixed-income instruments. This section illustrates some major swings in the market's valuation of the standard investment vehicles and the subsequent performances of those vehicles.

   Before examining the changes, we will examine benchmark performances. The data in Table 3 summarize the compound annualized return (including the reinvestment of interest and dividends) to four major categories of investments. Short-term Treasury bills, which carry neither default nor interest-rate risks, returned 3.5 percent over the sixty-three-year period. This yield just barely exceeds inflation. At the other end of the risk-reward spectrum, common stocks returned 10 percent and small company stocks yielded 12.3 percent.

Table 3. Annualized Returns to Standard
Portfolio Investments: 1926–1988[a]

Investment	Percentage Return
U.S. common stocks	10.0
U.S. small company stocks	12.3
Government bonds	4.4
Treasury bills	3.5
Inflation	3.1

[a] A period of sixty-three years was used because the standard financial data base published by Ibbotson Associates uses 1926 as its base year.

Source: Ibbotson Associates, Inc., Chicago, 1988.

These results may or may not be repeated over the next sixty years. We doubt they will, but whether they are repeated is not relevant: Few portfolios have the luxury of a sixty-year horizon. The ability to meet the needs of the portfolio beneficiaries—a university endowment, an employee's future retirement plan, or an individual's current income needs—is significantly affected by shorter-term investment results.

Table 4 demonstrates that there have been substantial variations in relative returns among asset categories for long periods in the past thirty-nine years.

The twenty or so years after World War II were ideal for equity investors. Inflation averaged only 2 percent, and stocks began the period incredibly undervalued. In 1950, the dividend yield on stocks was 8.8 percent, the price-to-book value (that is, the market value of the stocks compared with the total equity in the firms) was 110 percent, and the price-to-earnings ratio (market value of the stocks to total net earnings)

Table 4. Annualized Returns to Standard
Portfolio Investments for Selected Periods

	Return (%)		
Investment	1950–1968: The Golden Era of Common Stocks	1969–1981: The Era of Inflation	1982–1988: The Era of Financial Assets
U.S. common stocks	14.7	5.6	17.2
U.S. small company stocks	18.9	10.2	13.8
Government bonds	1.0	3.6	16.1
Treasury bills	2.7	7.3	7.8
Inflation	2.2	7.8	3.6

Source: Ibbotson Associates, Inc., Chicago, 1988.

was 10.5. These bargain-basement valuation levels were the result of a twenty-year adjustment from the pre-crash peak in 1929. The ravaging that equity investors took in the 1930s, a decade when investors lost money from start to finish, created an enormous aversion to stocks. The fear of equity ownership was so great that investors demanded an 8.8 percent current dividend yield on common stocks before they would change from Treasury bonds with a yield of only 2.2 percent!

Conventional academic wisdom suggests that a period of low inflation should produce attractive bond returns. Such was not the case in the 1950–1968 period, when long-term government securities returned only 1.0 percent per year, including the coupon. The problem, of course, had nothing to do with inflation theories, but it had everything to do with valuation. The fear of losing money in stocks increasingly sent investors scrambling to bonds. So by 1950, the 2.2 percent yield on government bonds provided no premium for inflation even though it would average only 2.2 percent over the next nineteen years.

Markets do not value assets irrationally forever. The 14.7 percent annual returns for stocks and the 1.0 percent return for bonds were partly the result of a rational change in relative valuation. They also resulted from two other factors: government policies that kept liquidity plentiful (thus laying the groundwork for the inflationary period that followed) and investor psychology. Markets are seldom in long-term equilibrium, primarily because it is difficult to predict the long-term economic, inflationary, and financial environments. Trends tend to strengthen, persist, and then reverse. During the process, assets tend to travel from one valuation extreme to the other.

Table 5 summarizes the dramatic change in equity and fixed-income values between 1950 and 1968. For each of the first three measures— dividend yield; price of stocks relative to book value (that is, equity); and the price of stocks relative to earnings per share—there was a sizable shift in market valuation between 1950 and 1968. In 1968, stocks were obviously more desirable to investors than they had been in 1950. Simultaneously, bonds became less desirable as illustrated by the higher yields they had to pay.

Table 5. The Valuation Cycle: 1950–1968

Measure of Value	1950	1968
Dividend yield	8.8%	2.9%
Price-to-book value[a]	110.0%	230.0%
Price-to-earnings ratio[b]	10.5	20.0
Treasury bond yield	2.2%	5.9%

[a]Market value of the stocks compared with the total equity in the firms.
[b]Ratio of the market value of the stocks to total net earnings.
Source: The Leuthold Group, 1988.

The policies of the 1960s that enabled the stock market to achieve new highs sowed the seeds of the inflation that occurred in the 1970s. After the postwar golden period for common stocks, conventional wisdom strongly predicted that equity returns would always swamp those of competing assets. Unfortunately, the thirteen-year period from 1968 through 1981, when inflation averaged 7.8 percent, was very bad for long-term financial assets. Returns on overvalued stocks that yielded only 2.9 percent and sold for a lofty 230.0 percent of book value in December 1968 failed to match the rate of inflation. Not surprisingly, at the outset of this period in 1968, prognosticators suggested that fixed-income investments had no place in portfolios and that equities should compose the bulk of one's assets. In fact, the Ford Foundation issued a report on college endowment policies in 1969 that urged institutions to invest more aggressively in equities. Many colleges and universities blindly followed that advice and regretted it a few years later.

During the thirty-two years through 1981, investments in the lowest quintile of market capitalizations (such as small stocks) provided superior performances: they returned 15.3 percent in contrast to 10.9 percent for the stock market as a whole. Since most active nonbank investment managers typically have a larger proportion of smaller capitalizations in their portfolios than do their larger competitors (such as banks and insurance companies), it was not surprising that the smaller independent investment advisors performed better than did their larger counterparts. Predictably, assets moved from the larger to the smaller investment advisors. By mid-1983, smaller capitalization equity valuations were higher than at any time since 1929.

This period influenced the allocation of assets immensely when investors looked backward. This environment in which three-fourths of the managers beat the Standard and Poor's (S&P) 500 spawned the huge proliferation of investment entrepreneurs. The conventional wisdom prevailing at that time was that smaller capitalization equities would always outperform larger issues.

Something else was changing as the bull market for small stocks was peaking. Fifteen years of escalating growth in money supply, double-digit inflation, and a sinking dollar forced a dramatic change in monetary policy in October 1979. The Federal Reserve Board decided to stop flooding the world with dollars, and the era of disinflation began.

The shrinking of liquidity resulting from monetary tightness took its toll on the markets. Treasury bond yields shot up to 14 percent by early 1982, and the stock market endured its first real bear market since 1973–1974. Relative valuations had changed dramatically by mid-1982, as shown in Table 6. The prevailing investor attitudes in mid-1982 assumed inflation was still a problem, one should never own a bond because they had lost money over the past thirty years, and stocks were terribly expen-

Table 6. The Valuation Cycle: 1968–1982

	Mid-1968		Year End, 1982	
Measure of Value	Value	Percentile Ranking[a]	Value	Percentile Ranking[a]
Dividend yield	2.9%	98th	6.0%	12th
Price-to-book value[b]	230.0%	97th	110.0%	12th
Price-to-earnings ratio[c]	20.0	90th	8.0	2nd
Treasury bond yield	5.9%	13th	13.7%	1st
Inflation rate (previous 12 months)	4.7%		8.9%	

[a]Lower numbers reflect degree of undervaluation since 1926 for stocks and 1970 for bond yields.

[b]Market value of the stocks compared with the total equity in the firms.

[c]Ratio of the market value of the stocks to total net earnings.

Source: For percentile ranks, The Leuthold Group, 1988.

sive with interest rates hovering around 14 percent. The mood represented a 180-degree shift from the euphoria surrounding the market peak in 1968. Table 6 shows the enormous change in relative valuation that had taken place over thirteen years. Yet, beneath the gloom was a sound economy. The three-year period of tight money and mounting investor pessimism had generated substantial declines in both stock and bond prices. With inflation heading below 3 percent in a few years, stocks selling at valuation levels that had been attractive only 10 percent of the time over the past fifty-six years and bonds yielding the highest values ever, the outlook for financial assets had never been better.

The annualized returns between 13 and 18 percent over the past seven years for both stocks and bonds (see Table 4) were unprecedented. Moreover, all major categories of financial assets, including Treasury bills, generated positive inflation-adjusted returns. Only one major category, small-capitalization equities, failed to perform as conventional wisdom would have predicted. In fact, although the 13.8 percent annualized returns bettered their sixty-two-year performance, these returns were a rather large 340 basis points (3.4 percent) per year below those of the S&P 500.

This underperformance of smaller equities severely affected the returns of most active managers. As mentioned above, the proliferation of new investment management firms resulted from the success of professional investors in generating returns better than those of the S&P 500 in the 1970s. In turn, most of those managers benefited enormously from the bull market in smaller capitalization equities during that same time. Suffering from the "live-and-die-by-the-sword" syndrome, the vast majority of managers failed to beat the S&P target in the late 1980s. Indeed, only 27 percent of the professionally managed portfolios were able to generate returns better than the S&P 500.

Why did smaller-capitalization equities produce returns below those of the larger companies? The answer lies only partially in the changes in relative profitability. The overvalued dollar suppressed the returns on equity of the manufacturing and technology sectors. However, the relative overvaluation of smaller equities in 1968 had a far greater impact. Figure 3 tracks the price-to-book value of smaller-capitalization equities relative to that of the S&P 500. Clearly, the relative valuation of smaller-capitalization stocks was at the upper end of its historical range in 1982 and continued to climb to its all-time high of 220 percent in 1983.

The seven-year bull market in financial assets has significantly changed equity and fixed-income valuations, as shown in Table 7.

To determine the appropriate strategic asset allocation (*strategic* implies a trend lasting at least five years), one must combine the outlook for inflation and the economy with the relative valuations for the major asset categories. (As discussed in the first section, we believe that monetary and fiscal policies are back on a disinflationary path, albeit a bumpy one.) On the valuation side, stocks seem to be a bit on the expensive side in the late 1980s, particularly relative to bonds whose yields are in the upper 10 percent of their 200-year history. On the other hand, smaller-capitalization relative multiples are at the low end of their historical range (see Figure 3).

The point of this brief financial history is to demonstrate the following three observations: market valuations do vary, the variations are significant enough that they can distort historical risk-reward balances, and

Table 7. The Valuation Cycle: 1968–1982

| | Mid-1968 | | Year End, 1982 | |
Measure of Value	Value	Percentile Ranking[a]	Value	Percentile Ranking[a]
Dividend yield	6.0%	12th	3.0%	82nd
Price-to-book value[b]	110.0%	12th	247.0%	95th
Price-to-earnings ratio[c]	8.0	2nd	16.5	62nd
Treasury bond yield	13.7%	1st	8.8%	8th
Inflation rate (previous 12 months)	8.9%		4.8%	

[a]Lower numbers reflect degree of undervaluation since 1926 for stocks and 1970 for bond yields.

[b]Market value of the stocks compared with the total equity in the firms.

[c]Ratio of the market value of the stocks to total net earnings.

Source: For percentile ranks, The Leuthold Group, 1988.

**Figure 3. Smaller-Capitalization Universe
Relative to S&P 500 (as of May 1989)**

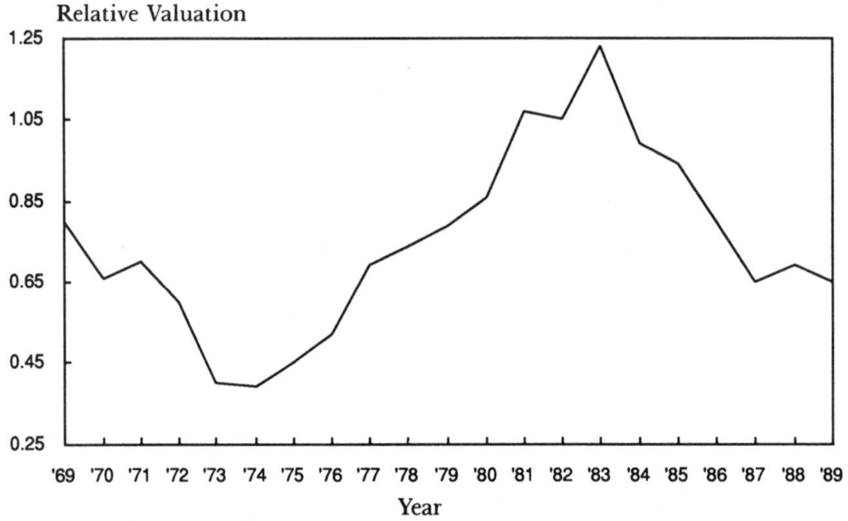

Relative Valuation

Year

the variations can be detected and interpreted in a timely manner. College and university financial managers can benefit from understanding and using such an approach.

How Useful Is New Information? Critics concede that this asset-allocation method has merit. But now that it has been articulated, they assert, the markets will anticipate portfolio re-balancing and discount the information. This may be true, but the markets have apparently not embraced SAA as fully as the theorists might expect. For example, a look at the experience of balanced accounts in the universe of pension fund managers demonstrates that a freshly awakened Rip Van Winkle would find the world, presumably re-defined by asset allocation, looking pretty much like it did when he dozed off. The line on Figure 4 indicates that the relative weighing of bonds and stocks in balanced funds has not moved very far from the norm during the 1980s. It appears, therefore, considerable room still exists for adding value to portfolio management with this type of approach.

Conclusion

The world economies are linked more closely than ever before. Events in one economy can affect and be affected by events in another. The stability of the U.S. economy is dependent, to a large extent, on the confidence of foreign investors. At present, the major sectors of our economy—government, consumers, and corporations—are overloaded with debt. At the

Figure 4. Balanced Funds: Average Annual Commitment to Equities (Years Ending June 30)

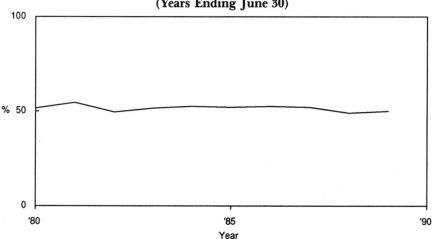

Source: SEI Corporation, copyright 1989. Reprinted with permission.

same time, we have been underinvesting in plant and equipment and in the public infrastructure. We have been consuming instead of producing and borrowing instead of saving. These excesses will be wrung out of the system, probably through market corrections. In such an environment, the financial skills of college and university managers will be tested.

In addition, the United States is no longer the undisputed economic leader of the world. The economic growth rate of Japan, for example, outpaces our own by a wide margin. The economies of many smaller nations are also expanding faster than our own, while the prospect for an economically united Europe in 1992 calls into question standard investment assumptions. Finally, the number and variety of investment possibilities has increased dramatically. In this environment, the most successful financial managers will extend their investments well beyond the U.S. borders and beyond the typical array of public and private debt and equity securities.

Strategic asset allocation is an approach that reduces risk and increases returns. SAA helps bring order to this panoply of options by blending strategic analysis with a quantitative/historical perspective. College and university financial officers should understand this technique if they expect to compete successfully in the challenges of the 1990s.

References

Benchmarks. Minneapolis, Minn.: The Leuthold Group, 1988.
Ibbotson, R. G., and Sinquefield, R. A. *Stocks, Bonds, Bills, and Inflation* (SBBI),

1982. Updated in *Stocks, Bonds, Bills and Inflation 1988 Yearbook*™. Chicago: Ibbotson Associates, Inc., 1988.

SEI Funds Evaluation Services. Wayne, Penn.: SEI Corporation, 1989.

Timothy Dalton is president of Dillon, Read Capital, Inc.

Kenneth Greiner is a senior vice-president at Dillon, Read Capital, Inc. He joined the firm after serving as a senior portfolio manager at the College Retirement Equities Fund.

Colleges and universities can borrow techniques from large financial organizations to protect both sides of their balance sheets.

Asset-Liability Management in Higher Education: Lessons from the Financial Markets

Aaron S. Gurwitz

As several authors in this volume make clear, the coming decade is likely to be characterized by market volatility and corrective actions. In Chapter Two, Murray specifically notes the extreme responses that could possibly occur. This chapter examines the mechanisms through which financial organizations protect themselves from these excesses.

Colleges and universities, with large financial assets and liabilities, may borrow the protection techniques used by large financial intermediaries. As with any insurance, this "hedging" carries some cost. But properly conceived and executed, these methods can be relatively inexpensive and save colleges millions of dollars if the markets turn against them.

In the current environment, in which funds flow across national boundaries with great ease, any protection from financial swings must be designed with an eye on trends in the global financial markets. In turn, emerging trends in international credit markets cannot be understood except by reference to the changing incentives facing major participants in those markets. In particular, the driving force behind many recent innovations has been efforts by financial intermediaries. (Financial intermediaries include the so-called thrifts [savings banks, savings and loans, credit unions]; commercial banks; mutual funds; brokerage houses; investment banks; pension funds; and insurance companies.) These intermediaries try to reduce the exposure of their net investment income to large shifts in yields and prices.

Colleges and universities in general, and large private institutions in particular, can be viewed as partially leveraged financial intermediaries. That is, these institutions are both borrowers from and lenders to financial markets. As Table 1 indicates, the sector as a whole is a net lender/investor, with net investment income accounting for approximately 4 percent of total revenues in 1986. While this net revenue was modest, it was still sufficient to defray most of the average four-year private institution's expenses for student services or for libraries and "public service" combined.

While a falloff in net investment income would probably not be devastating for a typical institution, it would be troublesome. Moreover, some colleges and universities have considerably larger endowments and/or are more highly leveraged with debt than most. College and university finance officials, particularly those at institutions with large endowments or debt, should be interested in the concept of asset-liability management for three reasons. First, specific applications of asset-liability management might help some institutions reduce the risk associated with their financial position while maintaining or increasing net investment income. Second (and probably more important), college and university officials are active participants in financial markets, and they must understand the opportunities and risks generated by the actions of large financial intermediaries trying to reduce their exposure to market volatility. Third, on occasion colleges and universities will undertake specific activities for which these techniques have particular relevance.

This chapter will discuss the general asset-liability management problem faced by major participants in financial markets: banks, thrifts, insurance companies, and pension funds. A summary will be given of some of the methods these institutions use to reduce their asset-liability risks at minimal cost to foregone net investment income. Another section will trace some of the impacts of these methods on financial markets in general. In the final section, the focus will return to the asset-liability

Table 1. Endowment Income, Mandated Expenditures, and Total Revenues for Private Four-Year Institutions of Higher Education[a]

Year	Endowment Income	Mandatory Expenditures[b]	Net Investment Income	Total Revenues	Net Investment Income as % of Total Revenues
1983	1,432	316	1,116	26,876	4.2
1984	1,543	356	1,187	29,493	4.0
1985	1,736	411	1,325	32,216	4.1
1986	1,860	442	1,418	34,953	4.1

[a] Amounts are in millions of dollars, except in column 6 (in which entries are percentages).
[b] Mandatory expenditures include primarily debt service appropriations, most of which is interest expense.

Source: U.S. Department of Education, 1987.

risks typically faced by colleges and universities. The techniques in this chapter are particularly relevant for institutions trying to protect themselves from extreme economic dislocations described in Chapter Two.

The Asset-Liability Problem

Financial intermediaries face a fundamental problem. They borrow funds at one interest rate and lend the money at a different rate. If the rate paid on the leveraged institution's liabilities rises relative to the yield on its assets, net investment income falls. If rates on both sides of the balance sheet are volatile and imperfectly correlated, the intermediary's profitability will also be volatile. Given investors' aversion to risk, volatile profits reduce the market value of a profit-maximizing firm. For a leveraged not-for-profit intermediary, volatility in net investment income limits the institution's ability to plan its future. Intermediaries can reduce the volatility of net interest income by borrowing and investing at highly correlated interest rates. For example, an institution might issue three-month floating-rate notes pegged to the London interbank offer rate (LIBOR) and invest the proceeds in three-month commercial paper. However, this "risk-free" strategy seldom produces sufficient profits.

The risks of an asset-liability mismatch have always been a problem for financial intermediaries. However, the problem has gotten worse during the 1980s for several reasons. Consequently, over the past few years, institutions have developed a wide variety of investment instruments and strategies, all of which have been aimed at controlling the impact of market risk on net investment income with minimum sacrifice of profit. The introduction of these instruments and implementation of these strategies has, to a large extent, conditioned the evolution of financial markets during the 1980s.

Although efforts to reduce the riskiness of intermediation at minimal cost to net investment income are not new, several developments have increased the impetus behind these efforts in recent years. The most important of these was the October 1979 change in the operating practices of the Federal Reserve Board. Before that date, interest-rate stabilization was one of the chief objectives of monetary policy. Since then, other objectives—such as stable growth of money supply, lower inflation, adequate nominal growth of gross national product (GNP), and solvency for third-world debtors—have become relatively more important than keeping interest rates from fluctuating too widely. As a result, interest rates have fluctuated over a much wider range during the 1980s than they had in previous decades. As Chapter One makes clear, stability is not likely to return to the markets in the near future.

The impact of past fluctuations on some financial intermediaries was devastating. The effect was particularly severe on thrift institutions. Savings and loan companies (S&Ls) and savings banks had always been in the business of taking in short-term deposits and lending the proceeds out as thirty-year home mortgages. The risk inherent in this strategy— that short-term deposit rates might rise above the yield on the mortgages—had always been present, but in an environment of interest rate ceilings on deposits and modest rate fluctuations, heavy losses had been unlikely. During the early 1980s, however, greater interest-rate volatility and deposit-rate deregulation combined to force some thrifts into severe losses. Healthy thrift institutions responded to this challenge by paying much closer attention to the risks inherent in their asset-liability positions and by adjusting their operations to minimize these risks.

In addition to thrift institutions, many insurance companies were hurt by the growing interest-rate volatility as they found they were holding low-yielding tax-exempt bonds at a time when they did not need tax-exempt income. Finally, the Employment Retirement Income Security Act (ERISA) required major corporations to pay much closer attention to the adequacy of pension funding. The wide fluctuations in market rates during the 1980s produced substantial shifts in the net surplus or deficit of assets over liabilities of many pension funds, with consequent impacts on the financial condition of the sponsors of the pension plans. Efforts by insurance companies and pension-plan sponsors to minimize the impacts of or in some cases to exploit these fluctuations in asset and liability values have become a major force in financial markets.

Methods of Asset-Liability Management

The process of asset-liability management begins with an assessment of the financial position of the institution under a wide range of interest rate and economic scenarios: slowly rising or slowly falling rates, rapidly rising or rapidly falling rates, a steepening or flattening yield curve, a rise or fall in real as opposed to nominal interest rates, and so on. (*Yield curve* refers to the relationship between interest rates and period of debt. During most periods, long-term liabilities pay a higher interest than short-term liabilities—a positive yield curve.) Usually, this assessment will reveal that net interest income or net surplus is much lower under some scenarios than under others, and that under some circumstances the institution is placed in serious financial jeopardy. For example, a typical thrift institution might face serious losses if the yield curve substantially inverted (that is, if short-term rates rose above long-term rates) because the income of these institutions is more closely tied to long-term rates while their costs (payment to depositors) are linked to short-term rates. By contrast, if interest rates fell sharply, a "young" pension fund with a large volume of short-term investments might find the discounted value of its liabilities rising faster than the market value of its assets. Falling real interest rates also might jeopardize an insurance company holding short-term investments and facing rising casualty claims; this was a major cause of the rapid increase in liability insurance premiums in the early 1980s.

The objective of asset-liability management is to adjust the financial structure of the institution to reduce or eliminate risk, and to make that adjustment at the lowest possible cost in either payments made or income foregone. To accomplish this goal,the asset-liability manager has a wide variety of tools at hand.

Matched Funding or Cash-Flow Matching. The oldest method of reducing risk is to match as closely as possible the maturities (or durations) of assets and liabilities. Thus, for example, S&Ls funded with short-term deposits might choose to hold only adjustable-rate mortgages (ARMs) in order to reduce the risk that the cost of funding might rise above the yield on investments. Or a pension-fund sponsor anticipating few expenses in the short run but large liabilities twenty years in the future might weight its portfolio heavily toward long-term zero-coupon bonds. The insurance company threatened by falling real rates might concentrate on inflation-hedge investments such as stocks, real estate, and commodities.

This method of asset-liability management (called *matched funding* or *cash-flow matching*) can, however, be a costly approach. In efficient capital markets,the yield spread between investments and liabilities with similar interest-rate sensitivities and similar liquidity and credit quality is usually quite small. In general, therefore, any net interest income generated by the matched funding either involves credit risk, nonliquidity, or both. Furthermore, the matched-funding approach is an imprecise tool; it protects the institution from the potential adverse effects of all interest-rate changes. It also eliminates the benefits of all changes. However, most institutions can easily withstand the impact of small interest rate shifts and stand to benefit under a number of scenarios. The most serious threats, however, are usually confined to a relatively small number of extreme circumstances. Consequently, financial intermediaries (and colleges and universities) can gain financial advantage if they do not try to "purchase" complete shelter but use hedge vehicles to protect against extreme risks.

Hedge Vehicles. The second approach to asset-liability management—the use of a variety of hedge vehicles—can be a less costly and more precise tool for managing asset-liability risk than the traditional matched funding or cash-flow matching technique. Hedge vehicles include a wide range of securities and contracts, such as futures contracts, options, interest rate swaps, and interest rate caps (see Exhibit 1). In general, institutions can change the interest rate profile of their net interest income or net surplus without changing the structure of either their assets or liabilities by buying or selling hedge vehicles. For example, a

Exhibit 1. Commonly Used Financial Hedge Vehicles

Hedge vehicles were created to protect merchants and farmers against volatility in the markets for their products and the raw materials for their trade. For example, hog farmers could sell "pork belly" futures contracts to protect themselves against a plunge in hog prices. Meat-packers, on the other hand, could purchase "pork belly" contracts, to protect themselves against a rise in the price of hogs. In the relatively recent past, these concepts have been adapted to the financial markets.

A *futures contract* is a contract to sell or purchase a financial security, type of security, or an equivalent "market basket" of securities at a specific future date at a specific future price.

An *option* is the right, but not the obligation, to buy or sell a specified security at a specified price on or before a specified date.

An *interest rate swap* is an agreement between two parties to exchange periodic cash payments at regular intervals. One party's payments are usually fixed, and the other's payments vary with some interest rate index. If one party holds debt with fixed interest payments and the other holds an equivalent amount of debt with variable interest payments, an interest rate swap can be effected to reverse those liabilities. That is, the party holding variable-rate debt can eliminate its exposure to interest rate fluctuations and the party holding fixed-rate debt can assume that risk.

The term *interest rates caps* refers to an agreement whereby one party, for up-front consideration, pays another party at specified intervals an amount proportional to the rate at which a specified interest rate index exceeds a specified level. If it does not exceed the level, no payment is made. In effect, a party that holds variable-rate debt can indemnify itself against excessive interest rate increases by purchasing an interest rate cap.

bank funded by short-term deposits and invested in intermediate-term corporate loans—and therefore exposed to higher interest rates or an inverted yield curve—could reduce this risk in a number of ways. It could, for example, sell U.S. Treasury note futures contracts. If interest rates rise, the profit earned on the sale will supplement the relatively low interest earned on the intermediate-term corporate loans. (At the same time, the bank will be paying a higher interest to depositors.) If interest rates fall, the bank will have a loss on the sale of the Treasury note futures but will have locked in a good rate on the corporate loans. The trick, of course, is to determine just the right amount of protection needed. Other ways of achieving this protection are to buy put options on U.S. Treasury notes or note futures, to enter into an interest rate swap contract (agreeing to pay a fixed rate and receive a variable rate payment), or to buy an interest rate cap.

As with matched funding or cash-flow matching, using hedge vehicles to the extent that all interest-rate risk to net investment income is eliminated will (in efficient markets) reduce profits to the level that just compensates the institution for credit risk and nonliquidity. However, hedge vehicles offer two advantages over matched funding. First, adopting a large hedge position is usually more efficient transactionally than restructuring an asset or liability portfolio. Second, hedge positions can be designed to deal with an institution's exposure to specific scenarios, so the use of hedge vehicles is a more precise tool for asset-liability management than either matched funding or cash-flow matching.

"Tailored" Assets and Liabilities. The final method for managing asset-liability risks involves the creation of new varieties of investment securities or financing vehicles specifically designed to alter the overall risk profile of a financial intermediary. The process of tailoring new varieties of assets and liabilities has been developed most fully in the home mortgage market. The risk profile produced by leveraged investments in mortgages and mortgage-backed securities can be particularly complex because mortgagors retain the option to prepay their loans at any time, usually with no penalty paid to the lender. The general problem faced by an S&L is, as described previously, that they finance long-term mortgage investments with short-term liabilities. Thus, S&Ls face the risk of losing a lot of money if the yield curve inverts while interest rates are rising. However, S&Ls, which derive a large proportion of their income from the fees charged for servicing mortgage loans, might also be threatened if interest rates fall sharply. In that event, the mortgages serviced by the S&L will be refinanced and prepay sooner than expected, and the anticipated stream of mortgage-servicing income might never be realized.

One way in which S&Ls might deal with this problem would be to invest in hedge vehicles, such as call options, which would perform particularly well if interest rates fall sharply but would not make matters worse for the institution if interest rates rise. Another option would be to invest in assets that would turn in an adequate return if interest rates remain close to current levels or rise somewhat, but would perform especially strongly if rates fall sharply and mortgagors begin to prepay more quickly than anticipated.

One such investment is a principal-only (PO) mortgage strip. This instrument is created by separating the interest and principal payments on a underlying pool of mortgage loans into separate securities. The PO strip pays no coupon, but the investor receives all the scheduled and unscheduled payments of principal on the pool. Like all zero-coupon securities, POs are sold at a discount to par. If the underlying mortgagors prepay faster than expected at the time of original pricing, the investor will receive the par amount faster than expected, producing a high total return. Therefore, investments in POs, which will perform especially well if mortgagors prepay rapidly, can act as a hedge against unanticipated decreases in an S&L's mortgage-servicing income.

This third approach to asset-liability management often offers more risk reduction at lower cost in terms of foregone net investment income than does either cash-flow matching or the use of hedge vehicles. The new securities, created by arranging the cash-flows of existing instruments, are frequently worth substantially more in market value than the single security from which they were derived. The value added will be largest when all the separate new securities provide solutions to the specific asset-liability problems faced by individual institutions.

For example, in the case of mortgage strips, the PO portion can, as described above, help reduce the risks faced by institutions that derive a large proportion of their income from mortgage-servicing fees. At the same time, the interest-only (IO) strips might be ideal investments for S&Ls who derive relatively little income from servicing mortgage loans but hold large portfolios of fixed-rate, long-term, mortgage-backed securities. The net income of these institutions would, therefore, perform poorly if interest rates rose sharply. IOs do especially well in a high-interest-rate environment, when prepayments are unexpectedly slow and interest payments on an outstanding pool of mortgage loans last longer than anticipated. If some investor is willing to pay top dollar for the IO strip, then the price of the PO could be quite reasonable, and the S&L specializing in mortgage servicing might be able to achieve the desired risk reduction with little or no sacrifice of asset yield.

In addition to the potentially lower cost of tailored assets and liabilities, this approach to risk management offers the additional benefit of regulatory and accounting treatment that is more advantageous than is treatment of certain hedge vehicles. Most intermediaries are subject to strict regulations, which frequently limit the degree to which such vehicles as futures and options can be used. In other cases, accounting standards may force institutions that use these vehicles to realize gains or losses on the hedge at more frequent intervals than the asset or liability portfolios are marked to market. Under these accounting standards, the use of hedges can actually add to the volatility of reported net investment income, even while the hedge strategy may be reducing the riskiness of economic income. Therefore, in many cases, tailored assets and liabilities may be preferable to hedge vehicles for noneconomic reasons.

Impacts on Financial Markets

A number of changes in the structure and performance of financial markets in recent years can be traced directly to efforts by financial intermediaries to ameliorate the effects of market volatility on net investment income. And colleges and universities, as participants in these markets, must be aware of these forces.

One of the most visible effects (one that has received much attention since the collapse of stock prices in October 1987) has been the rapid growth of markets for hedge vehicles. The volume of trading in interest rate futures and options contracts has grown rapidly through the 1980s, as has the volume of stock index futures and options. Part of this growth reflects a speculative demand, but a large part of the open interest represents the use of these contracts to hedge the asset and liability portfolios of the intermediaries. The growth of hedge markets has exerted an independent impact on the markets for the underlying cash securities. The availability of a viable, liquid hedge market has made bond dealers more willing to hold substantial inventories of securities and has, thereby, enhanced the liquidity of the cash markets. At the same time, the opportunities for arbitrage across the cash, futures, and options markets occasionally may have increased the daily volatility of securities prices.

The volume of transactions in exchange traded futures and options contracts represents only the tip of the iceberg of hedging activity. For example, the volume of interest rate swaps outstanding has grown from near zero ten years ago to $700 billion early in 1989. As is the case with exchange-traded hedge vehicles, activity in the interest rate swap market has created arbitrage opportunities in related cash, futures, and options markets. In many instances, the specific structure of new corporate bond issues can be understood only by the realization that the combination of the issuer's new liability with interest rates swaps and/or over-the-counter options will produce a low all-in-cost and a desirable risk profile.

These examples indicate that all active participants in financial markets, whether or not they actually use hedge vehicles, must be armed with at least some understanding of the workings of hedge markets and their impacts on securities markets.

General Implications for Colleges and Universities

These developments have two broad implications for colleges and universities in their role as partially leveraged financial intermediaries. First, the techniques of asset-liability management offer opportunities for any leveraged, or partially leveraged, financial intermediary to improve balance sheet performance. The issue probably will become more important to universities in the future since the tax law has imposed limitations on aggregate use of tax-exempt financing by private colleges and universities. The process of assessing risk and then choosing the most precise and effective methods for reducing risk can help raise net investment income and/or reduce the potential volatility of net investment income.

Consider, for example, a typical private university with a large endowment and a somewhat smaller debt position. Suppose that the outstanding debt is largely in the form of seven-day variable-rate demand notes (VRDNs) and that the endowment portfolio is invested in high-grade, fixed-income securities with an average maturity of ten years. Such an institution is in roughly the same risk position as the typical savings and loan institution: liabilities are much shorter than investments. If interest rates rise sharply, the institution's net interest income might drop or disappear. (Of course, most institutions include a large proportion of stocks in their endowment portfolio. But these equities are unlikely to protect earnings because the stock market usually falls when interest rates rise.) If the risk is severe enough—for example, an increase of 200 basis points (2.00 percent) in the VRDN would reduce net investment income to zero, and any greater increase would result in a net loss—then the institution might consider taking some steps to reduce the risk. The most drastic step that could be taken would be to match the interest sensitivity of assets and liabilities by, for example, fixing the rate on the VRDNs for the remaining term to maturity or by shortening the average maturity of the endowment portfolio. Alternatively, the institution might assume a partially hedged position by, for example, purchasing an interest rate cap that would help ensure that net investment income would remain positive, even if the VRDN rate rose by more than 200 basis points. Or the university might seek out a tailored investment or combination of investments that offer a fixed return if interest rates fall or rise by less than 200 basis points, but then begin to offer higher returns as interest rates rise above that level.

Colleges and universities are only partially leveraged financial institutions. For those with relatively little debt outstanding and/or relatively small investment portfolios, the business risks associated with interest rate volatility may not be terribly important. The second major implication of this analysis applies to these institutions as well as the more highly leveraged universities. The developments in financial markets attributable to asset-liability management on the part of major intermediaries can offer substantial opportunities for portfolio performance to investors who are not leveraged. In particular, the development of new varieties of assets designed to ameliorate the risks facing typical intermediaries often involves the creation of financial byproducts. For example, the creation of IO mortgage strips as the ideal investment for the typical thrift institution also produced PO strips as a byproduct. Strong demand for IOs led to the availability of large volumes of unsold PO strips offering very attractive yields. Similarly, the stripping of U.S. Treasury securities, which was undertaken mostly to fill the demand for long-dated zero-coupon assets, created large volumes of coupon strips with shorter maturities. In order to clear the market, these byproducts (shorter-maturity coupon strips) had to offer much higher yielded than securities of comparable riskiness.

Investors who are unconstrained by specific asset-liability problems can benefit from the constraints that face other institutions. Of course, buying PO mortgage strips or Treasury coupon strips may create changes in the risk profile of an investment portfolio that require additional hedging or asset rebalancing. However, currently, the key to above-average performance in fixed-income market is the ability to understand the dynamics of asset-liability management of major types of financial intermediaries and to exploit the byproducts of that process.

Finally, colleges and universities may engage in special projects for which these techniques and the related market understanding are particularly important. Efforts to help families finance tuition or a faculty mortgage assistance plan are two obvious examples. In such cases, these techniques can be specifically applied to protect the financial integrity of the projects.

Reference

U.S. Department of Education. Office of Education Research and Improvement. Center for Education Statistics. *Bulletin: Current Funds, Revenues, and Expenditures in Institutions of Higher Education: Fiscal Years 1983–1986.* Washington, D.C.: U.S. Government Printing Office, 1987.

*Aaron S. Gurwitz is a vice-president and senior economist
in the Economics Department of Goldman Sachs & Co.
He also has served as senior economist at the Federal
Reserve Bank of New York.*

As we enter the 1990s, states are particularly vulne   n
economic downturn. Policymakers will, however, lo   to
higher education to support state economic growth.

The Outlook for State Support
of Higher Education

Steven D. Gold

State governments play a critical role in financing higher education. Their appropriations are the largest single source of funds for all higher education. Although the bulk of these funds goes to public institutions, trends in the support of public higher education have inevitable consequences for private higher education as well. By analyzing state support for higher education in the recent past as well as the outlook for the next decade, this article can help college administrators anticipate the financial environment in which their institutions will operate in the 1990s.

State spending on higher education is more than $60 billion per year, making it the second largest component of state budgets. (Only aid for elementary and secondary schools is greater.)

This chapter focuses on the outlook for state support of higher education over the next decade. It is organized into three parts: the major relevant trends during the recent past, the outlook for state finances in general, and the prospects for higher education. The analysis in this chapter is at the national level, virtually ignoring the major differences that exist in trends from one state to another. Although interstate variations are important because states are not uniform, there is also a value in describing broad national trends since they reflect developments in many individual states and also highlight policy concerns from a federal prospective. This chapter deals solely with state support of higher education and does not consider changes in local government funding.

The views expressed are the author's and do not reflect the position of the National Conference of State Legislators.

The Past Decade

Although this chapter is specifically about higher education, it is necessary to consider trends that are occurring in the entire state budget. Because higher education is such a major component of state spending, general state fiscal conditions are the most important determinant of state support for higher education.

Trends in State Finances. State fiscal conditions have been volatile over the last ten years—very good in the late 1970s, very poor in the early 1980s, then improved in the mid-1980s (but not as good as they were in the 1970s) (Gold, 1988b, pp. 284-307). Fluctuations in the health of the national economy and changing state tax policies are of primary importance in explaining these trends. Spending policies have followed rather than led the deterioration and improvement in fiscal conditions. Cutbacks in federal aid were a negative factor affecting the fiscal condition of the states, but they were considerably less important than economic trends and tax policies.

The best way to gauge the fiscal health of the states is to track their year-end balances, especially the sum of their General Fund and Rainy Day Fund balances expressed as a proportion of General Fund spending. The year-end balances represent reserves that can be tapped in the future, a kind of safety net. When they diminish as a proportion of annual spending, the margin of protection against unexpected problems is reduced. These balances were as high as $11.8 billion in fiscal 1980 (9 percent of spending), but they plummeted to just $2 billion in 1983. Then the national economic recovery and state tax increases boosted balances to $9.7 billion (5.3 percent of spending) in 1985. In the following two years, balances slipped to about $7 billion and then rebounded in 1988 to $9.8 billion (4.2 percent of spending) (Howard, 1989).

The past year was a particularly quiet one for budgeting in most states because the national economy has been stronger than expected, causing revenues to somewhat exceed the projections used when budgets were enacted. California, Massachusetts, and New York are exceptions to this generalization in that they experienced unanticipated revenue shortfalls related to the transitional effects of federal tax reform on capital gains realizations. Most other states avoided such problems by utilizing more conservative assumptions in projecting revenue (Gold, Eckl, and Fabricius, 1988).

Table 1 shows how state tax revenue has fluctuated as a proportion of personal income during the 1970s and 1980s. Contrary to widespread perceptions, state taxes in 1989 are close to their all-time peak as a proportion of personal income. The tax revolt of the late 1970s along with the recessions of the early 1980s caused state taxes to drop relative to personal income, but they have now rebounded to $7.02 per $100 of

Table 1. State and Local Tax Revenue in Dollars per $100 of Personal Income, 1970 to 1987

				State				
Fiscal Year	Total	Local	State	General Sales	Personal Income	Corporation Income	Severance	Other
1970	11.32	5.07	6.29	1.86	1.20	0.49	0.09	2.65
1971	11.50	5.26	6.27	1.88	1.24	0.42	0.09	2.64
1972	12.24	5.51	6.77	1.99	1.47	0.50	0.09	2.72
1973	12.41	5.43	7.01	2.04	1.60	0.56	0.09	2.72
1974	11.93	5.16	6.81	2.07	1.57	0.55	0.11	2.51
1975	11.74	5.09	6.68	2.07	1.57	0.55	0.15	2.34
1976	11.98	5.17	6.85	2.10	1.65	0.56	0.16	2.38
1977	12.15	5.17	7.02	2.14	1.77	0.64	0.15	2.32
1978	12.08	5.01	7.10	2.21	1.82	0.67	0.16	2.24
1979	11.37	4.46	6.94	2.19	1.81	0.67	0.16	2.11
1980	11.02	4.26	6.78	2.14	1.84	0.66	0.21	1.93
1981	10.85	4.20	6.67	2.07	1.82	0.63	0.28	1.87
1982	10.59	4.12	6.49	2.01	1.82	0.56	0.31	1.79
1983	10.68	4.25	6.46	2.02	1.88	0.50	0.28	1.78
1984	11.30	4.35	6.96	2.21	2.09	0.55	0.26	1.85
1985	11.28	4.34	6.97	2.25	2.06	0.57	0.23	1.86
1986	11.24	4.37	6.89	2.26	2.04	0.55	0.19	1.85
1987	11.48	4.48	7.02	2.26	2.16	0.59	0.12	1.89

Note: The national total does not equal the sum of state and local taxes because personal income of the District of Columbia was excluded in calculating state tax revenue per $100 of personal income. It was included in calculations of total and local tax revenue per $100 of personal income. For that reason the "total" does not equal the sum of local and state revenues.

Sources: For tax revenue: U.S. Census Bureau, *Governmental Finances in 1970 through 1987*, 1971–1988; U.S. Census Bureau, *State Government Finances in 1970 through 1987*, 1971–1988. For personal income: U.S. Department of Commerce, 1987.

personal income, which is not far below the all-time peak of $7.10 in 1978.

Taking a longer perspective, one can see that state taxes as a percentage of personal income are at the top of the range in which they have fluctuated since 1973. Also, states have taken a much more prominent role in financing services by assuming a significant share of the burden that used to be borne by local governments. Because local tax revenue has fallen so much relative to personal income, combined state-local tax revenue in 1987 was 5.5 percent below its 1977 level and 7.5 percent below the all-time high in 1973.

A significant caveat is necessary concerning the 1987 tax revenue reflected in Table 1. The large increases in personal and corporate income tax revenue in 1987 compared with 1986 are partially a response to federal tax reform. Many investors realized capital gains in anticipation of the increase in the maximum federal tax rate from 20 percent to 28 percent, and many corporations accelerated state tax payments because they were more valuable as federal deductions before the federal corporate tax rate fell from 46 percent in 1986 to 40 percent in 1987 and 34 percent in 1988. Relative to personal income, revenue from both kinds of state income taxes certainly fell in fiscal year 1988, although national statistics for that period are not yet available.

Consideration of nontax revenue (such as federal aid and user charges) is important also, but considerable care is necessary to avoid misinterpretations. As Table 2 shows, data on state general revenue show a small increase relative to personal income between 1978 and 1987 despite a small decrease in tax revenue and a larger drop in federal aid. The major reason for the increase in total general revenue is the huge rise in miscellaneous revenue, which virtually doubled as a percentage of per-

Table 2. State General Revenue in Dollars per $100 of Personal Income, 1970, 1978, and 1987

Category of Revenue	1970	1978	1987
Total[a]	10.19	11.85	11.93
Federal aid	2.52	3.14	2.71
Taxes	6.29	7.10	7.02
Charges	0.80	0.85	0.91
(Higher education)[b]	(0.46)	(0.47)	(0.51)
Miscellaneous	0.45	0.55	1.09
(Interest)[c]	(0.19)	(0.28)	(0.54)

[a]Local payments to state governments are excluded.
[b]Higher education is a subcategory of Charges.
[c]Interest is a subcategory of Miscellaneous.

Sources: U.S. Census Bureau, State Government Finances in 1971, 1979, and 1988; U.S. Department of Commerce, 1987.

sonal income during this period. This miscellaneous revenue increase overstates the growth of resources available to states because about half of miscellaneous revenue is interest received. Although the growth of interest received partly reflects a rise in interest rates and improved cash management, it also is due to a trend toward creative financing (to realize arbitrage earnings, among other reasons) that led both interest received and interest paid to grow at extraordinary rates. Also, much of the increase in interest received (and paid) represents activities such as housing and economic development that are separate from General Funds and have no bearing on core state programs such as higher education.

Several other aspects of Table 2 are important to note:

• Federal aid to states fell about 14 percent as a proportion of personal income between 1978 and 1987. This is considerably less than the federal aid decrease experienced over this period by local governments (from $1.21 to $0.55 per $100 of personal income, a 55 percent decrease) because the most vulnerable federal programs were those that began following the Great Society initiative of the 1960s. Just as federal aid to localities grew much faster than aid to states from 1965 to 1978, so it fell much faster in the retrenchment period that followed. Figure 1 contrasts the large rise and decrease of federal aid to local governments with the relatively small fluctuations in federal aid to states.

**Figure 1. Federal Aid to State and Local
Governments Relative to Personal Income**

Index (1978 = 100)

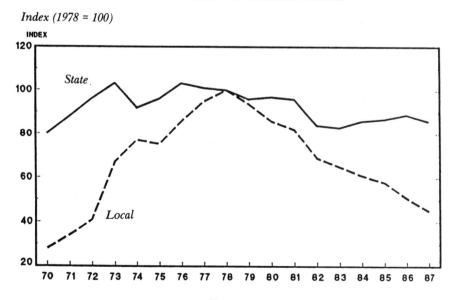

Year

• State revenue from charges has risen as a proportion of personal income but not by a great deal, increasing from 0.80 percent of personal income in 1970 to 0.91 percent in 1987.

• Higher education charges account for slightly more than half of total state revenue from charges and represented a fairly steady proportion throughout the 17 years. This implies that they too rose faster than personal income, but not by much.

Table 3 examines changes in state spending patterns from 1976 to 1987, once again relating the amounts to personal income. This analysis is important because it shows how higher education spending has fared in comparison with other categories of spending. Because this table incorporates data from several different sources, the figures for different categories of spending are not exactly comparable, but the methodology employed in developing the table is a good one for the issue at hand. For higher education, the table shows state appropriations, and for elementary-secondary education it shows state spending excluding federal aid passed through to local school districts. For other categories of spending, the table refers to general spending as reported by the U.S. Census Bureau, with federal aid subtracted. It does, however, include spending financed by user charges.

According to Table 3, higher education accounted for 10.5 percent of state spending in 1987. This is a low estimate because of the asymmetrical treatment of education and other expenditures in state budgets. If spending financed by charges were subtracted from health, hospitals, highways, and miscellaneous spending—as tuition, fees, and other miscellaneous revenue were subtracted for higher education—spending in those categories would decrease and higher education's share would corresponding increase.

Higher education appropriations decreased from $0.97 per $100 personal income in 1976 to a low of $0.90 in 1983 and 1984, and then it recovered slightly, rising to $0.92 in 1987. The percentage of total spending received by higher education also trended downward, starting at 11.3 percent in 1976 and reaching a peak of 11.9 percent two years later, before decreasing steadily to 10.5 percent in 1987.

The information in this table suggests that higher education received little if any benefit from the publicity in the mid-1980s about deficiencies in our education system and the perceived connection between higher education and economic development. Although higher education appropriations did increase faster than personal income from 1983 to 1986, its share of total state spending continued to decrease.

Table 3 indicates that state spending priorities have been gradually shifting. The two areas of strongest growth are Medicaid, which in twelve years rose from $0.35 to $0.58 per $100 of personal income, and correc-

Table 3. State Spending in Dollars per $100 of Personal Income, Excluding Federal Aid, 1976 to 1987[a]

Year	Total	Higher Education	Elementary-Secondary Education	Medicaid	Other Welfare	Health and Hospitals	Highways	Corrections	Other
1976	8.57	0.97	2.35	0.35	0.67	0.76	0.91	0.19	2.37
1977	8.33	0.96	2.28	0.38	0.60	0.77	0.77	0.20	2.37
1978	8.12	0.97	2.27	0.38	0.61	0.76	0.77	0.21	2.15
1979	8.11	0.94	2.30	0.42	0.50	0.75	0.79	0.21	2.20
1980	8.23	0.94	2.36	0.46	0.51	0.77	0.80	0.22	2.17
1981	8.27	0.93	2.28	0.48	0.52	0.80	0.71	0.23	2.32
1982	8.12	0.91	2.17	0.49	0.46	0.79	0.71	0.24	2.39
1983	8.14	0.90	2.16	0.56	0.37	0.79	0.67	0.25	2.45
1984	8.26	0.90	2.17	0.57	0.40	0.77	0.66	0.27	2.53
1985	8.44	0.92	2.23	0.56	0.37	0.78	0.65	0.30	2.62
1986	8.58	0.93	2.27	0.55	0.38	0.80	0.66	0.33	2.63
1987	8.77	0.92	2.28	0.58	0.37	0.80	0.72	0.33	2.77

[a]Data are derived from various sources, which may not be entirely consistent. A number of adjustments and corrections had to be made. For example, personal income excludes income from the District of Columbia because it is considered a local government by the Census Bureau. Spending for a fiscal year is divided by personal income in the calendar year that ends during it (for example, spending for Fiscal Year 1987 is divided by personal income in calendar year 1986).

Sources: U.S. Census Bureau, Governmental Finances in 1976 through 1987, 1977–1988, Table 2; for higher education appropriations, data reported by Illinois State University, The Grapevine, as reproduced in Wittstruck and Bragg, 1988, p. 49; for elementary-secondary education, National Education Association, 1988, and previous issues. Medicaid spending is from Medicaid SourceBook: Background Data and Analysis, 1988, supplemented by Census Bureau reports on city and county finances and unpublished information provided by the Health Care Financing Administration. Personal income is from U.S. Department of Commerce, 1987.

tional systems, which jumped from $0.19 to $0.33. Elementary-secondary education did not fare particularly well in the first part of the period, but state spending for it did increase somewhat as a proportion of personal income between 1983 and 1987, as the school reform movement swept the country. The magnitude of the increase is not, however, particularly impressive.

In attempting to infer state priorities from shifts in spending patterns, one should consider not just the amounts spent but also how needs were changing. For example, it might be concluded that, despite sluggish spending increases elementary-secondary education fared relatively well considering that enrollment fell 12 percent between 1975-76 and 1984-85 and increased only 1 percent in the next two years. Similarly, while enrollment in higher education was rising, growing 5.8 percent between 1976 and 1983, it did not increase nearly as rapidly as it had in the previous two decades, thereby reducing the need for new capital investments. Enrollment fell in 1984 and 1985 and rose only moderately in the following two years.

Table 4 places higher education spending in a different perspective by tracing changes in appropriations per student, taking inflation into

Table 4. State Appropriations for Higher Education per Student, 1973 to 1987

Fiscal Year	Nominal Spending (Dollars)	Inflation-Adjusted Spending[a] (Dollars)
1973	1,609	3,490
1974	1,791	3,561
1975	1,911	3,446
1976	1,987	3,309
1977	2,222	3,469
1978	2,452	3,574
1979	2,696	3,624
1980	3,025	3,691
1981	3,232	3,545
1982	3,420	3,537
1983	3,575	3,493
1984	3,814	3,555
1985	4,349	3,861
1986	4,695	4,001
1987	4,882	4,002

[a]1982 = 100 using a calendar year; the fiscal data are for fiscal years. Inflation is measured by the implicit gross national product deflator for state and local governments, with calendar years averaged to estimate each fiscal year.

Sources: For appropriations: Wittstruck and Bragg, 1988. For enrollment: Data provided by Jackie Johnson, Senior Policy Associate, State of Washington, Higher Education Coordinating Board. For inflation: U.S. Council of Economic Advisers, 1988, p. 253.

account. Real spending per student was virtually unchanged between 1973 and 1983, with sharp decreases in the recessionary period of the early 1980s wiping out the relatively small gains of the 1970s. There were, however, rather sharp increases in 1985 and 1986, representing a 12.5 percent total gain in those two years. These increases can be viewed either as a recovery from the cuts of the early 1980s or as a sign of higher education's stronger clout in the development of state budgets. The recovery explanation appears more warranted in view of the lack of a further increase in 1987.

Trends in Higher Education Finance. An important change in state higher education policy in the 1980s has involved increased reliance on tuition and decreased reliance on state appropriations. According to a study by the State Higher Education Executive Officers (SHEEO), from 1982 to 1988 tuition increases outpaced increases in state appropriations in five of these seven years. In contrast, in every year from 1974 to 1981, appropriations increased at a higher rate (Wittstruck and Bragg, 1988).

For the entire period from 1981 to 1988, state appropriations for higher education rose 62.6 percent while university tuition and state college tuition rose 93.3 percent and 91.7 percent, respectively. These SHEEO figures are somewhat biased in that they compare the total volume of appropriations (which reflects growing enrollment) with average tuition levels per student (which do not reflect any change in enrollment). This bias tends to overstate the reliance on appropriations per pupil relative to tuition, since enrollment rose 2 percent between 1981 and 1987. A better comparison is the 51.5 percent increase in appropriations per pupil between 1981 and 1987 versus the increases of more than 79 percent and 81 percent in the two types of tuition. (This comparison goes only through 1987 because enrollment data for 1988 were not available at the time of this report.)

This increased reliance on tuition also is reflected in U.S. Census Bureau data. Excluding auxiliary enterprises, higher education charges in 1981 covered 24.7 percent of current operating expenditures. By 1987, these charges covered 29.2 percent of current operating expenditures. From another perspective, higher education charges (excluding auxiliary enterprises) rose 88.5 percent from 1981 to 1987 while tax revenue increased 64.9 percent and operating spending not covered by charges increased 49.8 percent.

Most of the statistics presented in this chapter have placed state support of higher education in a somewhat unfavorable light by comparing increases with personal income, tuition, or tax revenue, each of which have increased considerably faster than inflation. State support appears more generous if it is compared with inflation itself. From 1981 to 1988, state appropriations rose 62.6 percent, far outpacing the Consumer Price

Index increase of 34.4 percent. In other words, real state appropriations have increased substantially.

To summarize, state tax revenue has risen slightly faster than personal income in the 1980s, and, in 1987, it represented nearly as high a proportion of personal income as it ever has. Higher education appropriations have been a relatively constant proportion of personal income in the 1980s, but they have fallen somewhat relative to personal income since the late 1970s. Real state appropriations per student have not increased strongly, except in 1985 and 1986 when states were recovering from the fiscal problems caused by the recessions of the early 1980s. State support for higher education has been adversely affected by strong competition for funds from Medicaid and corrections programs. Public institutions of higher education have relied heavily on tuition in this decade to compensate for the relatively slow growth of state appropriations.

Outlook for State Finances

The current relatively healthy appearance of state finances could change quickly if the economy deteriorated. As discussed above, the state fiscal situation was extremely depressed in the 1982–83 period when the economy was in recession. To a considerable extent, as the economy goes, so go state finances.

States would be in a much better position to weather a downturn in the economy if they held large reserve balances, but, in general, the reserves currently held by states are not sufficient to provide much of a buffer. According to the most recent survey by the National Conference of State Legislators of state fiscal conditions and budget actions, only eight states had a balance (including the General Fund and Rainy Day Fund) equal to at least 10 percent of General Fund spending at the end of fiscal 1988 (Gold, Eckl, and Fabricius, 1988).

Many casual observers of state finances have been misled by the proliferation of Rainy Day Funds (RDFs) in recent years. While thirty-one states now have these budget-stabilization funds on their books, most of them are not well funded. Total RDF balances at the end of fiscal 1988 were about $2.7 billion (that is, only about 1 percent of annual state spending). Moreover, to a considerable extent, RDFs have been a substitute for (rather than a supplement to) balances ordinarily held in the General Fund. Only three of the existing RDFs rely on a formula to determine when funds are added to or withdrawn from them, so there is little obstacle to raiding the fund at the first sign of budget difficulty.

The State of the Economy. Economists differ widely in their projections of the economic outlook. My own view is that our prosperity is rather precarious. The rapid buildup of our external debt is likely to slow down as foreigners become increasingly reluctant to finance our deficits. Unless we have extraordinarily able economic leadership, a high degree of coordination with our trading partners, and great luck, the fragile international economic system could impose serious strains on our financial system. Of course, it is possible to conceive of domestic policies that would effectively move us toward eliminating our trade and federal budget deficits, but it is doubtful that the political will exists to implement such policies. We need to shift resources away from consumption on a large scale, which will require strong economic leadership. Such leadership—which would convince the public to accept major sacrifices in the short run to ensure economic health in the long run—does not appear to be in plentiful supply.

State Tax Policy. Even if the economy avoids a serious recession, economic growth is unlikely to be robust since relatively little unused capacity is available and labor force growth will probably be slow because of demographic trends. This implies that the growth of state revenue will be relatively modest unless taxes are increased. If the fiscal behavior of the 1990s is like that of the 1980s, not many major tax increases are on the horizon.

Since the personal income and general sales tax account for more than 60 percent of state tax revenue, most tax initiatives designed to raise a significant amount of additional revenue rely on these two types of taxes. During the 1980s, the great majority of sales and income tax increases were enacted to avoid a budget deficit. The second most common rationale for increasing the sales or income tax was to finance an improvement in elementary and secondary school programs. Significantly, not many states did raise taxes for this reason, and those that did were all states with relatively low-quality educational systems in which the poor caliber of the schools was deemed to be an important economic development liability. In other words, very few states have had major tax increases in the 1980s except to avoid a deficit or to improve the elementary-secondary schools. This record does not provide much basis for optimism about the feasibility of raising taxes for some other reason, such as improving state services.

The majority of major state tax increases in this decade occurred in 1982 and 1983, accounting for the large jump in fiscal 1984 revenue that is apparent in Table 1. While income and sales taxes both were used heavily at that time, the aftermath of those increases has important implications for the future. Approximately three-quarters of the personal income tax increases in 1982 and 1983 were either partially rolled back or completely repealed as the fiscal health of the states recovered in 1984 and 1985. (Most of the sales tax increases, however, remained in effect.) Thus, many states did not retain the deficit-inspired tax increases once the specter of the deficit was lifted (Gold, 1988a).

There are two important reasons for the go-slow policy on tax increases in the 1980s. First, the legacy of the tax revolt endures. After Proposition 13 passed in California in 1978, it led to an initial round of tax cuts, and thereafter it inhibited states from raising taxes. Eventually, those inhibitions weakened, and most states did raise taxes in 1982 or 1983. The memory of the tax revolt does not stop all tax increases, but it does make it harder to enact them. The tax limitations and tax cuts inspired by the tax revolt (either through initiatives or legislative action) have also had a dampening effect on revenue increases in quite a few states. A second restraining influence is interstate tax competition, which has spurred on the trend away from highly progressive income taxes, has favored the trend to grant business tax exemptions for inventories and purchases of manufacturing equipment, and has hastened the demise of the unitary approach to taxing multinational companies.

The state response to federal tax reform also has some important lessons. Although states could have received an estimated $6 billion windfall if they had conformed to federal tax reform without changing their tax rates, most states with large potential windfalls did not follow that course. Consequently, only about one-fifth of the estimated windfall was received by states. States with relatively high tax rates tended to reduce them, and they and many other states with lower tax rates also avoided the windfall by boosting personal exemptions and standard deductions (Gold, Eckl, and Erickson, 1987; Gold, 1988a).

One notable result of many state tax reforms of 1987 was to reduce the elasticity of state tax systems. Because tax-rate structures tend to be "flatter" after reform, the automatic growth of revenue resulting from the growth of the economy will be less high than before reform in many states (Galper and Pollock, 1988).

While the reluctance to raise income tax rates and the reduction inelasticity have negative effects for future revenue growth, other developments are more favorable. States have shown less reluctance about raising excise taxes than in the past. This is reflected in Table 1 by the failure of nonincome, nonsales, nonseverance tax revenue (in the last column) to decrease as a proportion of income between 1981 and 1987, as it had tended to decrease in the past. Another favorable development is the increased interest in state tax reform (Gold, 1988c). Not only did most states respond creatively to the opportunity to improve their income taxes provided by federal tax reform, but they also have initiated a wave of tax reform that could help to strengthen their tax systems by broadening tax bases and rationalizing long-neglected tax provisions. One avenue that they are likely to follow in the 1990s is expansion of the coverage of the sales tax to services, although not necessarily to the extent that Florida attempted (and failed in its attempt).

Federal Aid and Tax Policies. A third development that could adversely affect the states in the 1990s is possible cutbacks in federal aid.

Although most Reagan administration proposals in recent years have not been successful, it is conceivable that the Bush administration might have more success in cutting spending as part of an overall effort to cut the federal deficit.

In viewing federal aid cuts, it is important to recognize that sometimes their indirect effects are more important than their direct impacts. For example, local governments might lose more than states directly, but states might then step in to assist localities. Similarly, federal cuts for social services or Medicaid might hurt education indirectly because state officials might consider it necessary to replace a large portion of the cutbacks.

Federal tax policy could also have adverse effects on the states. Many would consider a federal value-added tax a serious threat to state reliance on the sales tax. More likely, the federal government could rely heavily on increased excise taxes and further restrictions on municipal bonds as part of a deficit reduction package. Both of these policies would hurt state and local finances to some extent.

Summary. The outlook for state finances is hardly a rosy one. The economy is likely to perform considerably worse in the next decade than it has in the past five years. The ability to raise taxes is limited by the legacy of the tax revolt and intergovernmental competition. Federal deficit reduction could make things worse for the states. Even if the worst scenarios are avoided, the prospects for the next few years are not bright. Big increases in revenue appear highly unlikely.

Prospects for Higher Education

The first part of this chapter showed that higher education has not fared particularly well over the past decade in the competition for state dollars. The second section suggested that the outlook for state finances is not as favorable in the 1990s as it has been since 1984. The logical conclusion is that, unless something important changes, higher education cannot anticipate large new infusions of state dollars.

The great hope for higher education could be its link to economic development. State interest in economic development is still keen, and many believe that there is surely a relationship between economic development and higher education. The connection is not, however, a simple one and it has so far not been enough to bring in large amounts of new dollars to universities. In general, there often seems to be a lot more rhetoric about economic development than hard money to back up the talk. Although economic development is a favorite buzzword in state capitols and all sorts of programs wrap themselves in the mantle of economic development, it may be that its potency as a lever for obtaining state resources has been exaggerated.

The prospects for state-supported higher education are closely tied to the prospects for state finances in general. Increases in appropriations for colleges and universities are closely correlated with economic growth, which is the single most important factor determining fiscal health. It is probably just wishful thinking to expect higher education to start faring better in the competition for state dollars. At least as likely, state universities and colleges may fall behind as other interests make stronger claims.

References

Galper, H., and Pollock, S. "Models of Income Tax Reform." In S. D. Gold (ed.), *The Unfinished Agenda for State Tax Reform*. Denver, Colo.: National Conference of State Legislators, 1988.

Gold, S. D. "Developments in State Finances, 1983 to 1986." *Public Budgeting and Finance*, 1987, 7 (1), 5-23.

Gold, S. D. "Blizzard of 1987: A Year of Tax Reform Activity in the States." *Publius*, 1988a, *18* (3), 17-35.

Gold, S. D. "State Fiscal Conditions." In M.G.H. McGeary and L. E. Lynn (eds.), *Urban Change and Poverty*. Washington, D.C.: National Academy Press, 1988b.

Gold, S. D. (ed.). *The Unfinished Agenda for State Tax Reform*. Denver, Colo.: National Conference of State Legislators, 1988c.

Gold, S. D., Eckl, C. L., and Erickson, B. M. *State Budget Actions in 1987*. Denver, Colo.: National Conference of State Legislators, 1987.

Gold, S. D., Eckl, C. L., and Fabricius, M. A. *State Budget Actions in 1988*. Denver, Colo.: National Conference of State Legislators, 1988.

Howard, M. A. *Fiscal Survey of the States*. Washington, D.C.: National Association of State Budget Officers, 1989.

Medicaid SourceBook: Background Data and Analysis. Washington, D.C.: Congressional Research Service, 1988.

National Education Association. *Estimates of School Statistics: 1984-85* and *1987-88*. Washington, D.C.: National Education Association, 1985 and 1988. (2 editions.)

U.S. Census Bureau. *Governmental Finances in 1970* through *1987*. Washington, D.C.: U.S. Government Printing Office, 1971-1988. (18 editions.)

U.S. Census Bureau. *State Government Finances in 1970* through *1987*. Washington, D.C.: U.S. Government Printing Office, 1971-1988. (18 editions.)

U.S. Census Bureau. *City Government Finances in 1976* through *1987*. Washington, D.C.: U.S. Government Printing Office, 1977-1988. (12 editions.)

U.S. Council of Economic Advisers. *Economic Report of the President: 1988*. Washington, D.C.: U.S. Government Printing Office, 1988.

U.S. Department of Commerce. *Survey of Current Business*. Vol. 67. Washington, D.C.: U.S. Government Printing Office, 1987.

Wittstruck, J. R., and Bragg, S. M. *Focus on Price: Trends in Public Higher Education: Tuition and State Support*. Denver, Colo.: State Higher Education Executive Officers, 1988.

Steven D. Gold is director of Fiscal Studies for the National Conference of State Legislators.

Government and university leaders sometimes have trouble reaching agreements because they are so much alike.

Higher Education and the Federal Government

Suzanne H. Woolsey

The arguments and discussions presented in the previous chapters of this volume consist of a range of sophisticated and complex analyses of the external forces that affect university financial fortunes. The authors draw lessons from these analyses for university leaders in the assessment of risks and institutional resilience, and they arrive at rules for making decisions about the management of assets in times of economic uncertainty.

The four general types of analyses are as follows:

- An assessment of likely fiscal and economic policy changes and appropriate institutional hedges against the likely excesses of either inflation and recession
- A description of financial markets as they may change (and as they have changed in the recent past), and the appropriate institutional response to the uncertainties inherent in the markets
- An analysis, via the development of an econometric model of university and small college financial flows, of the relative importance of various external influences on the financial health of institutions
- A review of the present status and likely prospects for state government involvement in higher education, in terms of both funding and regulation.

The underlying premise of these chapters is that, despite considerable uncertainty (which is traceable to the prospective behavior of institutional investors), the hand of the federal government is immensely powerful in tightening or loosening the money supply, increasing or decreasing the size of the deficit, and increasing or decreasing the incentives for private savings and investment. They also make it clear that the blunt instruments of federal monetary and economic policy are difficult to control with sufficient precision to avoid unintended effects. These authors accurately perceive that government fiscal and economic policy-makers rarely lose sleep over the consequences of their decisions for universities (as compared with the manufacturing or financial industries, for example). The authors agree that universities not only must become better at reading the signals in order to anticipate trends but also must make more precisely calibrated hedging decisions, because governmental policy is not going to change for them.

Chapter One focuses on the overall economic outlook and its impact on college and university operations. Specifically, Anderson and Massy predict that in order to simultaneously maintain economic growth and satisfy foreign creditors necessary for survival in the global economy, the United States must shift from growth based on consumption and government spending to exports. This policy will trigger growth in business investment to continue the manufacturing boom that has already begun, along with cutting the federal deficit to avoid soaking up savings. This will probably be achieved through a combination of spending cuts and tax increases and will necessitate that the dollar remain weak to attract exporters.

In addition, efforts to increase tax revenues are already affecting colleges and universities; revenue generation devices often rely on such university-related items as higher tax action of unrelated business income, employer-subsidized education, and limiting availability of tax-exempt debt. Reductions in the deductibility of gifts may affect donations, and the proposed Treasury Department excise tax on the investment returns of endowments would obviously reduce net institutional revenues. The changeability of tax policy seems to be its only consistent characteristic.

In the second chapter, Murray suggests that planning must include an understanding of potentially extreme changes in the operating environment. To the extent possible, institutions should hedge against economic disaster of either hyperinflation or 1930s-style collapse. Although the effect will be strongly felt by the endowment fund, it is likely to extend as well to other aspects of institutional life, including the availability of bonds for capital expansion and public and private ability to pay instructional costs.

Chapter Four addresses the problems of investing in an uncertain economic environment. Dalton and Greiner project growth rather than reduction of the federal deficit. In light of the economic imbalances characteristic of a nation living beyond its means, they suggest attention to market forces as a key to prudent investment.

Whereas in past years the stock market has been driven by financial restructuring, the critical variables in the 1980s have become cash flow and quick payback, with little emphasis on long-term growth. Colleges and universities should take a long-term investment perspective, including technology stocks. While it appears that the worst of the liquidity squeeze has passed, rapid economic growth would bring back fears of inflation and send the values of the dollar, bonds, and stocks rapidly downward.

In Chapter Five, Gurwitz addresses asset-liability management in higher education institutions. In general, he defines colleges and universities as partially leveraged financial intermediaries that are both borrowers and lenders to financial markets. As such, asset-liability management based on an understanding of the opportunities and risks generated by a large financial intermediary will help institutional administrators reduce exposure to risk.

In 1979, the Federal Reserve Board adjusted its first-priority monetary policy from interest-rate stabilization to stable growth of money supply, lower inflation, and nominal growth of gross national product (GNP). Since then, interest rates have fluctuated widely. In response to the increased risks and in an effort to ameliorate the effect of market volatility on net investment income, financial intermediaries have developed tailored assets and liabilities that offer both reduced risk and cost to an individual institution. Given his definition of universities, Gurwitz suggests they use the same type of strategy.

Two other chapters approach the government role from a different angle. The chapter by Gold on state roles in university finance highlights the traditional state function of funding instructional costs at public universities, and it describes some recent initiatives by states to move into selective additional investments in university endeavors, particularly for economic development. Given the fiscal constraints of most states, Gold advises against university reliance on hopes for expansion or even absent-minded continuation of current levels of appropriation.

His assessment is that federal cutbacks in aid have worsened state fiscal conditions but are a less important influence than economic trends and tax policies. Gold suggests that in the future, the higher education community will likely be faced with direct cutbacks in federal aid as part of an overall effort to reduce the federal deficit. In addition, indirect effects will be felt as states struggle to compensate for cutbacks in other areas (for example, Medicaid) by diverting funds that might otherwise be spent on education. Finally, Chapter Six addresses the concern that federal tax policy could also create an adverse effect on state policies. For example, federal revenue-raising options could include a federal value-added tax, increased federal excise tax, and restrictions on municipal bonds. Therefore, Gold concludes that colleges and universities should maintain sufficient liquidity in their endowments to protect against this possibility.

In Chapter Three, Nordhaus constructs a model that estimates the fiscal vulnerability of institutions to risks associated with various external sources of financing; the most intriguing part of his analysis is the use of a volatility measure to add weight in the model to those sources of revenue whose levels vary dramatically and unpredictably from year to year. Such variations require additional management attention and contingency planning, and reliance on such revenue flows reduces the institution's resilience and ability to control its own destiny.

Nordhaus finds that larger universities generally are affected by shocks to the overall economy and government spending, while small colleges are influenced more heavily by internal factors (such as faculty salaries and tuition charges). A major difference between the two types of institutions is government support for life sciences, which has contributed to financial growth of research universities through rapid growth in support of biomedical research. By multiplying level of funds flow by volatility, Nordhaus finds that the most crucial factor for large research universities is the general level of federal appropriations to universities. Great volatility comes from government spending since a large part of the revenue for higher education comes from the federal government, which historically has provided a highly volatile spending stream. Furthermore, as the federal government struggles to reduce its deficit, funding for higher education will enter into a period of particularly high risk.

Understanding the Relationship Between Higher Education and the Federal Government

All authors of this volume demonstrate great sophistication in their respective disciplines, but they treat this federal monster as an unpredictable generator of independent variables for their analyses. I submit that a closer examination of the ways in which government entities impinge on colleges and universities may provide some useful insights.

A bewildering range of federal policies and federal actions have direct effects on universities, perhaps more than on any other (theoretically) nonregulated industry. These effects include the power of economic and fiscal policy decisions; the impact of variations in appropriations; and multiple regulatory and tax-related statutes, regulations, and court decisions. The range and volume of federal efforts at least partially cause educators' frustration in dealing with the federal establishment. However, an additional frustration factor on both sides of government-university relations differs markedly from the interactions of many other groups.

Watching these interactions over several years and from many different vantage points leads one to the belief that government and university leaders have difficulty getting along with each other in large measure *because they are so much alike.*

Similarities Between Government and University Organizations. Both the executive branch of the government and organizational structures of universities are extremely decentralized compared with other organizations, most notably those of highly centralized corporations. Decision-making processes are complex, with much effort given to developing consensus and making certain that all bases are covered. To ensure this, most administrations develop a White House office to coordinate policy development, and the Office of Management and Budget (OMB) has long performed a clearance function that concentrates solely on aggregating the positions of various parts of the government on an issue and highlighting any lack of consensus or deviation from previous policy. University committee structures serve an equivalent purpose inside their organizations.

In both kinds of organizations, it is extremely challenging to try to represent the position of the institution in a dialogue with external decision makers. This is true for structural reasons; these organizations consist of many different, nonparallel entities, each of which has its own culture, institutional history, mission, processes, and policies, and the central leader speaks with some trepidation for all the parts.

The internal divisions within one of these organizations are capable of absorbing virtually 100 percent of the time of all its leadership. This leads to two sorts of responses. Leaders are either frustrated and distracted by the friction of the daily squabbles, or they decide to ignore the internal divisions and deal with their own particular interests.

But human nature seems to require (perhaps for the preservation of optimism) that each individual firmly believe that the organization in which he or she is rooted is the only one that is muddled and mired in internal disputes. All seem to understand their own realities all too well, but they discount the possibility that others have similarities. For example, when negotiations between universities and government agencies become necessary, this trait results in two unfortunate outcomes:

- Both parties to the negotiation tend to assume the other represents an immensely more unified, goal-directed, and purposeful institution than their own.
- Any mixed signals, inability to deliver as promised, or backing away from tentative commitments is perceived as evidence of malice rather than confusion.

These misunderstandings are almost programmed into most government and university officials in their discussions with one another. They are perhaps further amplified by a certain belief on both parts that each is working in a dedicated way for eminently laudable goals. It is difficult to collide with another self-sacrificing, dedicated individual, also working for the greater good, who appears to be taking a position diametrically opposed to one's own.

Differences Between the University and the Federal Perspectives. The public good that is the focus of most federal effort cuts across the institutional interests of universities and is largely indifferent to its own effect on them. This is the case for two reasons: First, the scale of concern at the federal level on any issue is so broad that specific institutional effects are not part of the analyses; macro policy is the focus. Second, in the government (unlike Bauhaus architecture), function tends to follow form. That is, each of the many federal agencies that are important to higher education has its own interests, priorities, and culture.

The impact of this macro-view and force of form affects policies on higher education very directly. To colleges and universities, the nature of the debate appears to be off center, and the ensuing policies seem even incomprehensible or contradictory. The following examples may be helpful:

• The Labor Department and Education Department, representing manpower training specialists on the one hand and educators on the other, always have fought about what should be done in the general areas of vocational and technical education; postsecondary, community college; job training; and the learning part of a response to high-risk youth. Recent welfare reform legislation authorizes major new funds for the educational needs of welfare recipients, through the Labor Department and presumably state welfare agencies. And, at the present time, a large portion of the outlays for Pell grants to finance higher education for the poor are going to the technical, job-training, vocational programs that welfare-reform monies (to say nothing of already existing youth-employment and vocational-education programs) are also designed to fund. Despite years of research on how best to educate/train people for the work force, the overall structural questions are never answered because the issue always dies in the cross fire of the departmental turf wars.

• The institutional histories of the Defense Department, on the one hand, and Health and Human Services, on the other, have affected dramatically their willingness to consider the needs of organizations as vessels for federal funding and their treatment of those organizations. After World War II, the Department of Defense consciously invested in major research at universities in order to build the intellectual infrastructure. Some have said that the main thing the Department of Defense does when there is no war is to buy things, and it is accustomed to dealing with large corporate entities in partnership arrangements. Despite recent severe tightening of Department of Defense procurement rules, the underlying culture is one in which organizations outside the federal agency have been relied on to help further the national interest. Health and Human Services is, at heart, a welfare agency. It has two standard program forms: check-writing to individuals (Social Security, Medicare) and reimbursing states for part of their federally authorized expenditures on programs (aid to families with dependent children, social services). Such an organization develops a keen eye for individual cheaters and institutions that are trying to overcharge the federal government.

The different experiences of universities audited by HHS versus those overseen by DOD and can be tied to these very different institutional cultures. For years, there has been a bimodal distribution of university anger over OMB circular A-21; those for whom Health and Human Services was the cognizant agency were treated like potential welfare cheats, while the Department of Defense auditors tended to think of their "auditees" as somewhat irritating partners in national security.

• Policy decisions have never been coordinated between student aid programs (largely for undergraduates, funded through the Education Department) and the graduate research fellowship programs (funded through the National Science Foundation and the National Institutes of Health). The interface between the two is clearly not of concern for the managers of either set of programs. The chasm between the student aid and the research agencies was poignantly demonstrated soon after the passage of the Gramm-Rudman-Hollings deficit-reduction act. In the executive branch response, science agencies carefully exempted graduate fellowships from cuts, while the Education Department proposed major shrinkage of undergraduate student aid. When questioned on the inconsistency, neither agency had been aware of the policy of the other.

It is small wonder that overall volatility in federal funding for higher education is so high. But, given the destructive effect of that volatility on the institutions that are attempting to carry out the federal mandate attached to the funds (and carry out their other disparate missions of teaching, research, clinical care, community service, economic development, and professional training), understanding the nature of the variations may provide some help in minimizing the damage of the oscillations.

Apparent Federal Policy Trends. In the past few years, the most important policy changes regarding higher education have been outside the area of direct appropriations. The major volatility noted by Nordhaus occurred early in the 1980s, and since then there has been a relatively steady, marginally upward course for university appropriations. The two areas that have seen the most activity have been those dealing with tax policy (specifically the increasingly stringent treatment of tax-exempt entities) and the web of regulations that reaches across a broad range of activities.

The tax-writing committees of Congress, working with the Treasury Department, have been exceedingly busy since 1981. After the initial tax cut bill of 1981, which engendered a great deal of entrepreneurial activity by tax-exempt as well as taxable entities, there has been a steady pressure on and erosion of the tax benefits for exempt institutions. As Kaye Hanson (1989) of the Consortium of Financing Higher Education (COFHE) has stated, the great victories of higher education in this area have been in maintaining the status quo in the face of attempts to eliminate existing provisions. With unremitting pressure to reduce the deficit without increasing taxes, the search for revenue enhancement will continue, and reductions in exempt organization benefits (given their lack of relevance to the priorities of those committees) will undoubtedly continue.

Regulatory mushrooms have sprung up throughout the federal as well as state governments. The pending elimination of the waiver of mandatory retirement at age 70 has engendered review of pension plans and early retirement incentives and has improved measures of faculty productivity. A range of health and safety rules, although clearly designed to improve the campus environment, have mandated additional capital expenditures to renovate and retrofit facilities, as well as personnel costs to achieve such goals as enhanced security and assurance of a drug-free environment. In the past several years, campuses have been faced with a wide range of new regulations, including increasingly stringent procurement and immigration requirements (both of which are difficult and costly to implement).

The most important federal issue relating to higher education in the early 1990s, however, goes back to the heart of traditional federal involvement in higher education. The entire range of student financial aid programs is due for reauthorization in 1992. That year will mark the twentieth anniversary of the 1972 Higher Education Act, which established today's student aid programs. Nearly universal dissatisfaction has developed over the fundamental mechanisms by which these programs work, and a thorough reconsideration is beginning, with a wide range of interested parties—governmental, educational, and financial—represented.

Replacing some student aid programs in their entirety with National Service has been recommended in the proposed Citizenship and National Service Act (1989) by Senator Nunn and Congressman McCurdy. Designing student-loan programs that will encourage more students to stay in school has been recommended by Fred Fischer (1987) of OMB who suggests a graduation-contingent loan program, in which the loan is forgiven if the student stays in school through graduation. In view of the current teacher shortage, reinstatement may be considered for the loan forgiveness based on years of teaching (part of the original National Defense Education Act).

Rethinking basic student-loan programs provides the opportunity for government constituencies who have difficulty dealing with each other to hammer out an analytical, if not political, truce. It also challenges the whole range of institutions of higher education, who have been trying with somewhat limited success to design adequate financial-aid packages on their own, to grapple with the more macro issues of public access to education.

References

Fischer, F. "Graduation—Contingent Student Aid: Fighting the High Cost of Dropping Out." *Change,* November/December 1987.

Hanson, K. "Current Issues in Higher Education." Speech given at the Higher Education Key Leaders Meeting, Coopers & Lybrand, Alexandria, Va., May 1, 1989.

Nunn, S., and McCurdy, D. *Citizenship and National Service Act (Proposed),* (S. 3, H.R. 660). January 1989.

Suzanne H. Woolsey is executive director of the Commission on Behavioral and Social Sciences and Education at the National Research Council.

INDEX

Ordering Information

New Directions for Higher Education is a series of paperback books that provides timely information and authoritative advice about major issues and administrative problems confronting every institution. Books in the series are published quarterly, in Fall, Winter, Spring, and Summer, and are available for purchase by subscription as well as by single copy.

Subscriptions for 1990 cost $48.00 for individuals (a savings of 20 percent over single-copy prices) and $64.00 for institutions, agencies, and libraries. Please do not send institutional checks for personal subscriptions. Standing orders are accepted.

Single copies cost $14.95 when payment accompanies order. (California, New Jersey, New York, and Washington, D.C., residents please include appropriate sales tax.) Billed orders will be charged postage and handling.

Discounts for quantity orders are available. Please write to the address below for information.

All orders must include either the name of an individual or an official purchase order number. Please submit your order as follows:
 Subscriptions: specify series and year subscription is to begin
 Single copies: include individual title code (such as HE1)

Mail all orders to:
 Jossey-Bass Inc., Publishers
 350 Sansome Street
 San Francisco, California 94104

OTHER TITLES AVAILABLE IN THE
NEW DIRECTIONS FOR HIGHER EDUCATION SERIES
Martin Kramer, Editor-in-Chief